· PIG YEARS ·

· PIG YEARS ·

Ellyn Gaydos

Alfred A. Knopf · New York · 2022

THIS IS A BORZOI BOOK
PUBLISHED BY ALFRED A. KNOPF

www.aaknopf.com

Knopf, Borzoi Books, and the colophon are registered trademarks of
Penguin Random House LLC.

Library of Congress Cataloging-in-Publication Data
Names: Gaydos, Ellyn, author.
Title: Pig years / Ellyn Gaydos.
Description: First edition. | New York : Alfred A. Knopf, 2022.
Identifiers: LCCN 2021038086 | ISBN 9780593318959 (hardcover) |
ISBN 9780593318966 (ebook)
Subjects: LCSH: Gaydos, Ellyn. | Agriculture—Vermont—
Biography. | Farm life—Vermont.
Classification: LCC S521.5.V5 G39 2022 |
DDC 630.9743—dc23/eng/20211104
LC record available at https://lccn.loc.gov/2021038086

Jacket images: (morning glory) *Morning Glory* by Pierre-Joseph
Redouté / Bridgeman Images; (shovel, Mount Lebanon, N.Y.)
Shaker Museum, Chatham, N.Y.; (soil) xpixel/Shutterstock
Jacket design by Kelly Blair

Pig illustration by FrimuFilms/Shutterstock.com

Manufactured in the United States of America
First Edition

Contents

· DAYS OF HARVEST ·

· WINTER ·

Author's Note

This story started as notes I was taking on pigs, but if I was going to write about pigs I'd have to write about the moon too and the wild creatures at the perimeters of the pig pens and eventually my eye would follow the bees into flowers; all of it connected. At first I wished I could tell it as if I were a fly showcasing the world of a small farm through a wild compound vision: here would be a scene of a tomato ripening, there a piglet walking through the forest or a farmer fixing a fence, and I would be omniscient, buzzing at the margins. But I began to find that the prose was much influenced by my simple brown-eyed human gaze. I had just turned twenty-four and fallen deeply in love, I had little money, was a transient worker, and was increasingly afflicted with the desire to have a child. All of this became like a conversation with the fields, animals, and various towns that surrounded me.

I am not from a farming family. Nearly all of my relatives materialized in America during Ellis Island days and none refashioned themselves as agriculturalists. I was born in Vermont, a state that has an old-fashioned agricultural bent to it, old-fashioned because there's no great money to be made here and the farms are small, not like in the flattened Midwest, its expanse organized by tractors driven under the efficient eyes of satellites, or the ten thousand cow dairies in California that house neat rows of Holsteins. The most beautiful dairy farms here are on land that is too hilly for anything besides pasture, hills ensorcelled by gentle bovines with big wet brown eyes. As a child, I wanted to be a part of their society. Like many, I have chosen to make my money off nature. I am not a farm owner, so reliably I am paid by the hour. Most years I don't make it over the poverty line for a single woman. I could find a better-paying job if I wanted, and there is always enough food to eat. This is the compensation for the crude work of training life into channels of fecundity.

During my first farming job, at eighteen, I lived on a beef and vegetable farm two miles south of the Canadian border. I liked being subjugated to the farm there, bending beneath the unconcerned hand of work. In one half of the farmhouse, the older brick side, lived the French-Canadian grandparents, in the other their son and his family. I stayed in a trailer beneath the grain silo and tended the vegetables, never allowed to operate the tractor with a skull-topped gearshift. The grandfather, who had run the now defunct dairy, was relegated to mowing the lawn bald and maintaining a fleet of antique fire engines. The grand-mother picked whole wheelbarrows full of wild ramps and put up food. The children, two and five, roamed the farm wild while their parents worked. I bottle-fed a calf abandoned by her mother and we ate the negligent cow's heart in a thick stew.

The next summer I worked on a big berry farm, eating so many of the unsalable strawberries while I picked that I got sores in my mouth. Another summer I worked on a small dairy run by a seventy-year-old man. We milked cows in antique wooden stanchions and I lived in the tool shop. For health he ate raw beef culled from his herd for lunch. Mixed with onion it was deli-cious. He drove with a handwritten diagram chronicling the rise of industrialized food on the tailgate of his truck and would pull over to look at kestrels sitting in pairs of brown female and bluish male on telephone wires. He had the patience of an old man.

The following season, I found a job along the Winooski River, a few miles from where I grew up, growing vegetables in silty riverbank soil. Men with beards ran the farm for the most part. They specialized in carrots, grew so many we spent months picking, sorting, and washing, and in the last feet of carrots to dig they buried champagne so it would pop out of the ground like a final miracle. I kept my first pigs and in fall we made thousands of pounds of sauerkraut with our cabbages and sausage with the pork. I finished college and stayed a few seasons until the farm went bankrupt.

Apart from jobbing, I have always been somewhat embarrassed of myself, ashamed of wanting to be a writer. It is horrible to want to write well. As a child, I filled notebooks with poetry and became livid when anyone would ask about them. As an adult, I would rather be rewarded in eggplant or string beans for work performed. This, I think, is the kind of praise better fitting humans. That and the simple pleasure of laboring outside with its attendant sensations both plain and deep.

Amongst the plants and farmers, pigs are threaded through the narrative, pigs with admirable hardiness and observable tact husbanded year after year to the butcher. The crops of the field too must be laboriously tended, but the pig is something closer to a far-off verdant world, a sign of the earth's pull toward splendor. For this, I love a fat pig. These numerous pigs became favored personalities and came to represent a link between myself and the natural world. Reliably, they grew into symbols of fertility, good fortune even, as the seasons mounted. Their untimely deaths came with the cold, when they were handsomely fat and ready for slaughter. I've helped to raise many pigs and vegetables for the table. This repeated culling is an act of faith simultaneously in the continued fertility of the herd and the land. Faith in the continuance of things, of reaping and sowing, is necessarily invoked over and over again. Life is conjured and cut short. From cotyledons, those first hidden leaves enclosed in a seed, to florets of broccoli, from the thrust of a boar to a small and perfect piglet, all of it part of the flowering of the earth, its bloom and attendant rot.

Gumdrop

High Summer 2016, New Lebanon, NY

There is always other life on the sows, fallen elderberries stuck between coarse hairs, their seven-hundred-pound frames animated by the movement of green inchworms and errant piglets. M.J., in heat again, arrives panting before her midday bucket of cream. Her simple pig vulva has become full and dewy, a clean point of expectant flesh.

As she sucks in milk, the farmer's kids, towheaded in the sunlight, play on a mountain of shale in rain-soaked underwear. They wear homemade wire earrings that dig into their unpierced ears.

Gumdrop, one of the young meat pigs, is accidentally pregnant, upsetting the whole order of things. She was impregnated by a male smaller than her and late to be castrated. Her stomach has begun to round out into a home. *Does she know she is pregnant?*

Tina, the prima sow, is a falling star. Her hips have begun to show. She places her slack-jawed mouth on human keepers, an empty threat. Swollen with mastitis, only two out of sixteen nipples look full; the others hang loose. Piglets suckle at her to no end with secret pink tongues. Pigs have a three-month gestation with litters of up to fourteen. These four-year-old sows are both older and wiser than their keepers, who lamely facilitate the life of a domesticated animal that would happily care for itself in the wild. When they do manage to escape, they are adept at finding warm southern slopes in winter, acorn-laden woods in fall, and skunk cabbage, emerging in green spindles, from snowy spring woods.

I am the farmhand here, from spring until the cold weather comes, and I sleep in a house that has become a shared nest. In the summertime mice are born in the woodstove. I watch a milk snake wind across the bathroom floor behind a running mouse. A porcupine lives under the porch, nocturnally sawing at the foundation. On the way home from work on the farm, I drive five miles per hour behind a slow-waddling skunk and begin to worry that all these animals are making me soft.

A man and his girlfriend live across the driveway from me. The sign on their lawn reads IS THERE LIFE AFTER DEATH? KEEP GOING AND FIND OUT. He rides his motorcycle in the dark after his girlfriend gets home from work at the pound. In the grass circling their ranch house they keep an ancient Saint Bernard and a few goats with cancerous tumors that the girlfriend rescued from euthanasia. The goats' bleating in the woods sounds like human conversation.

Down the overgrown hill the farmer's towheaded children are now napping with a contagious cough. One of the younger pigs has a cough too, arching his long four-month-old back to expel. He is fed hemlock boughs in his grain bin as medicine. Another "grower" pig has earned the name Son of Chub Wub. When the first Chub Wub was slaughtered due to an untreated hernia, the farm children wept for their favorite pig, asking to be fed his heart in an act of compassionate consumption. Son of Chub Wub has extravagant jowls in thick red rolls around his jaw. He nursed from multiple sows as a baby and has grown fatter than all his siblings. A whole pasture was fenced in for them, only to be discovered as a private dumping ground, filled with trash bags and a broken sofa. The pen of adolescent pigs dug up a skein of barbed wire, nicking themselves on its dirt-colored gnarls of razor. The farmer's legs get caught in it, easily shredding his fine skin. The farmer is a quiet man. His wife tells me he mostly raised himself before they ran away together as teenagers, but he keeps a knife on the dashboard of his truck with a white handle made of antler, a gift from his father.

Expectant in July, Gumdrop has begun to produce milk. Her brothers and sisters have started losing their hair in the heat, but hers will grow in dark strands from now on, marking her as a mother. Gumdrop no longer lives with her siblings or the other sows but is alone in a wooded pen, waiting. The handlers approach her in swooping, nonpredatory arcs. Grain is poured on a stump for Gumdrop and her sawed-off plastic drum is filled with cow's milk.

When they are born, Gumdrop's babies are quite thin and look more simply *animal* than *pig*. They have the high hips of greyhounds and tails, not yet curled, that connote something rodent about them; their hooves and snouts have the infant elasticity of gummy bears. They came out like torpedoes all attached through different stems to one briny umbilical cord. With her long pig body, Gumdrop couldn't look over her shoulder to see them come out, each dressed in its own thin membrane. The guard dog ate the stillborn. Gumdrop's teats become her, swollen into licorice drops and beautifully productive. The fat on her back has melted away, almost by gravitational pull. She's very thirsty now and douses herself in mud. These day-old animals encircle her, searching her body, each with a set of eight needle-like "milk teeth." They huddle, the twelve of them, behind their mother, yelping when the girth of her crests their horizon. Nature, being unsentimental, accommodates the reality that some sows eat their young, but Gumdrop is gentle in her new domesticity, tenderly positioning her body so as not to squish anyone. She is a good mother.

Weeks later, we put Gumdrop's sons and daughters in a pen of ElectroNet adjacent to hers. They can no longer touch but they can still smell the cinnamon earth of one another and see the reds and blacks of each other's skin against sticks and dirt. Gumdrop is aggravated, but she has become exhausted with ensuring the twelve babies' survival.

The piglets are small enough to slide in and out under their electric fence. Turkey vultures watch them run across the shale field, a cluster of small ears in the wind. They are born adept at finding things, spilt grain or bottles of cream, white tubers growing in shaggy piles of shale, and feathery mushrooms sprouting on logs. They are allowed to roam free by mother sow and farmer alike, sometimes coming back with gashes across the big flesh of their noses, their finest sensory organs.

Eventually their ElectroNet is opened up. The farmer backs a horse trailer to their door and the piglets walk up a plank on new legs. The farmer drives down the dirt road, his blue truck towing them along as they scream, moving as they never have before. Their new home is a pen over open grass with an old billboard roof wrapped around PVC and chicken wire. The outline of the GEICO lizard grips on to the ceiling. There, underneath the car insurance ad, they will shuttle along, devouring acorns and dandelion buds.

One afternoon, we separate the boys from their sisters and file them back onto the trailer from whence they came. The farmer squats in a corner unwrapping the head of a scalpel and a bottle of iodine. When it has gotten quiet on the trailer, the pigs rooting through hay, he grabs a back leg of a forty-pound piglet. Kneeling opposite him, I get the piglet on his back, one leg pressed to the floor in each hand.

The farmer cuts through skin, then white fat and membrane. Beads of blood pearl around the scalpel as he does quick work. One testicle is squeezed through the incision. It is irregularly long, blue-gray, and attached by membrane on either side of its sac. The farmer pulls it out by its thin vas deferens, the hole left behind immediately filling with blood until it clots into a hanging mass. The other testicle is faster. Feces, urine, warm blood, milk feed, and animal stress choke the air in the trailer.

After all the males are operated on, none chosen to continue the lineage of their parents' Red Wattle–Mulefoot romance, I empty a bucket of testicles in the woods: a magnified pile of lima beans. The pigs return to their pen with gentle steps.

The rooster named Commander succumbs to the breeding of flies. He is under the care of the three-year-old. She puts black tar ointment underneath his wing where the flies are laying their eggs, rubbing her small black-polished finger in the pink crevice where they've cleared Commander's feathers out while his primordial yellow eyelids rise and fall. Before his wound he would charge down paths in the woods at his keepers, a free-roaming protector. She's keeping him in a cage, locking the door with a stick, and refilling his bowls of corn and water. Commander isn't getting better. One day the farmer takes him out of his cage and cuts his head off with a shovel, another compassionate act.

The kids still have the box turtle they caught in the murky pond behind their house and keep it as a pet. The boy fills his tank with rocks and leaves. He feeds him chunks of banana, attracting flies to their shared room. When I swim in the pond, I let the three-year-old put her arms around my neck, her white hair bobbing above the brown water. Afterwards, we sit on rocks like turtles ourselves to dry off in sun.

At a barbecue down the road that afternoon, a mechanical spit is plugged into an extension cord. The cook stands watching the young pig turn. Its backside of thickly muscled hams is throwing off the revolutions of the spit, causing it to gain speed around turns and thrust the pig facedown above the flames halfway through its mechanized revolutions. The cook motions to his son, positioning him with a stick next to the browning body. "Now," he says. His son jams the stick underneath the pig's ribs while he unplugs the extension cord, leaving the pig to cook on its back.

Because of her unexpected healthy litter, Gumdrop is allowed to outlive the meat pigs. She doesn't see her kids anymore, but she is bred again the next spring along with the other sows. Four months later, the piglets will come, unseen at first, though she already knows the points of their baby teeth and the warmth of their new rodent bodies. I watch the wordless way it happens the first time, life reproduced prescriptively and yet with astonishing delicacy.

As their replacements are born, every Wednesday pigs are taken away for slaughter. The farmer brings me the unsalable pieces to eat. I butcher the heads of three red pigs for their cheek meat, lifted by leathery ears and sawed away at on my kitchen table. I place each medallion of jowl into a Ziploc bag and peel away the white gristle that helped to bind the face together. I dig a hole in the woods and place the three cheekless heads in it. An iron eagle from a discarded woodstove serves as their grave marker with goldenrod and daisies laid across the eagle's talons. Is it an act of desecration to bury heads together like that?

I take the farm kids to the Doggy Dazzle show at the town library. A woman in blue eye shadow dances to KC and the Sunshine Band with her border collie, holding a paw in each hand. The collie runs through long cloth tunnels underneath the show tent. She herds him away into her car, the windows covered in strips of aluminum, and walks out a partially paralyzed corgi named Star. Objects are scattered across the ground. "Toothpaste," the doggy dazzler says. Star picks a tube from the ring, carrying it to the doggy dazzler in her mouth. "Remote," she commands. Star runs, her back end scooting across the ground in orange bounds.

The farmer and his wife are out late catching escaped pigs. On top of the shale field the power steering on the blue truck goes. The sky is almost white with stars. A part of the family for this fleeting season, I sleep on their couch in case the towheaded children wake up in the night.

The pigs are caught and the daylight remembers thimble-sized strawberries surrounding my cabin, each chewed to its red essence by birds and bugs. Elderflowers scent the farmer's yard and hang around the fence like wedding veils.

· First Bloom ·

New Lebanon

Summer's Eve 2017, New Lebanon, NY

Sometimes, from the corner of my eye I think my boss is a butterfly, or rather a butterfly is my boss. Peripherally, she is the quick turn of a cabbage moth in wind. But it is just Alice with a baby carriage, struggling through the shaggy uneven field, a white shade cloth flying around her carriage.

The farmers here are newlyweds, Alice, thin boned and green-eyed, and Henry, slightly fat on pork, with short unkempt hair and a beard of the same auburn. They have a baby and a freshly mortgaged house, two mutts, no wedding rings, and a field of pigs. It is a small farm made up of a fenced-in, sloping hill, less wild than Gumdrop's home.

Carved out of one side of the hill is a series of plots that makes up Alice's market garden. The rest is open pasture portioned out for the pigs. All around the hill, the neighbor keeps hayfields. Across the road is a freight rail line, which fills up once every workday with train cars piled with lumber. It is the focal point on the farm's horizon, that and the woods opposite.

They grow pattypan squash, something I have never seen before, a thick yellow star with the knowing weight of flesh and seed. On my first days working for them in spring, we shovel out the winter pig shed. The bedding, when prodded with a pitchfork, separates into dirt and straw and dust, which lifts into my mouth and onto the hairs of my eyebrows. Henry thinks there are a few stillborn piglets in the shed but amidst the animal ruts and leached straw, I find nothing. On the table we'll use to wash vegetables for market, bags of human breast milk lie scattered.

Fifteen minutes from Alice and Henry's small pig farm, the town of New Lebanon appears as singular strip along Route 20, a town easily missed. Reach into the console of the car, look up, and you've already come to the lone blinking stoplight, after which there is not much except spaced-out houses and a dumpster factory, but further on stands the Lebanon Valley Speedway, the grandest thing to be seen from the road—a dirt track surrounded by rough concrete walls that keep stock cars from flying onto Route 20 and cement bleachers that could be the walls of a castle. Seasonally, at the summer town board meetings, weekenders and second-home owners, mixed amongst the trailer park residents, farmers, hippies, and senior citizens, make an appeal to reduce operations at the track and make it quieter in town, but they never win. Local sympathy remains overwhelmingly with the speedway.

The downtown strip before the blinking light consists of little more than his and hers barbershops, a Family Dollar, China City Restaurant, a gas station, cafe, diner, an empty bowling alley, library, three churches, and two bars, on opposite sides of the road. The mountains are low and leveled off. There are billboards and chain stores with half-stocked shelves.

In its humble attire, this place does not give up its secrets easily.

For my lunch break, the general store offers a meatloaf special, served hot or cold, whichever way you like. It is heated on a home stove wedged in a corner behind the lunch counter. Pasta salad, an especially good one with tuna and peas mixed in, is scooped out from Tupperware onto a plate. All of it is served by the motherly proprietor, wearing a hairdo requiring considerable talent, who gives off the impression that this is also her home.

After she prepares my lunch she sits, perched on a stool behind the counter, delicately eating ice cream out of a teacup. It looks like butter pecan. She's moving to Arkansas in a few weeks to start a beef farm and shutting this place down. EVERYTHING MUST GO. She and her husband won't need to raise pigs out there 'cause there are so many wild boar to catch and eat. They will slaughter the animals on the farm, but she doesn't know if she can do it.

"People say that's what they're here for, at least some do. If we didn't kill them then they'd overrun us," she says.

I have two farm jobs this season. Half the week I go to Henry and Alice's pig farm, the other half to the vegetable farm run by my old friends Ethan and Sarah, both slight and dirty, elfin almost. Ethan has light hair and pink lips set against a deep tan cast by the summer sun of farm fields or the winter sun of woods where he fells trees. Not shy, but so soft-spoken that he must take on a falsely deep voice over the phone so that the person on the other end can hear him. Sarah has dark, closely trimmed bangs, the square jaw of her father, and big white teeth. Both have blue eyes that seem to refract the warm ember of sun so frequently invading them.

We live together in a small yellow house surrounded by yellow flowers. Goose, a large Maine coon that can dissect a mouse leaving only a single string of intestine attached to disembodied pink nose, lives there too. The house is not on the farm, the land belonging not to Ethan or Sarah but to the Sufi commune. The farm is a ten-minute drive down the road from our home, past cornfields, cows, and the diner. We return from work stinking of fish fertilizer, our boots and collars dirt laden. Most nights we eat rich vegetable-filled suppers at the kitchen table before collapsing into bed. I learn to sleep through the sounds of Goose crunching bones.

The Sufis began their commune in the 1970s, replacing the Shakers who had come before them. Every Wednesday there is free lunch. It is either a ploy to attract more members, an act of charity, or both. The chef is a beautiful woman with wild white hair. Her current boyfriend is in a rock cover band and I've seen her dancing to his music at the bar. She cooks meals for whoever wants to come. Her food is redolent of a health store buffet: lentils and rice, vegetable-rich soups, corn bread, jam bars, and giant bowls of salad with homemade tahini and green goddess dressings. Mostly in attendance are people from the road associated somehow with the commune, older and moved into their own houses, given up on true communal living.

The dining hall, which the Shakers constructed in 1831 for their own meals, is painted a cheery shade of yellow bordering wide planked wooden floors. There's a framed picture on the wall of the original communards, ragged and young, with visiting Shaker sisters, in dark bonnets, a shadow of the six hundred Believers who once lived here. By 1947 they were all gone, having let go of thousands of acres of farmland, seed and herbal tonic businesses, schools, a chair factory, and a tannery.

One of the final visitors to the Shakers was Berton Roueché, a young reporter for *The New Yorker,* who found a rather strange conglomeration of individuals, six women and one man, aged sixty to ninety-two, "lonely, retrospective, and gently backslidden," in an oversized boardinghouse. The remaining members seemed to suffer from both old age and pride. The last brother, Curtis, was found carrying a bucket of chicken feed from the barn and professed to the reporter, "Work made me well. Used to be I'd milk twenty cows and cut a cord of wood every day ... been cutting wood over forty years and lost only two toes. Wasn't my fault neither time." Later Roueché was brought indoors by the sisters and proudly shown a sixty-year-old talking parrot and a music box, amongst other accoutrements not associated with the monastic life but perfectly acceptable as comforts to the aged and lonesome. Long after the Shakers left, fire burnt the roof off their great stone barn.

Today, there are fewer and fewer Sufis left at the commune, an emptiness that carries an almost historical sense of inevitability; others say the mountain and these lands themselves exert a kind of magnetic pull and we are all arrived because of it. In spite of the past failings, young people still come here with communal hopes. I don't feel idealistic, belief not changing the work, the plain needs of the vegetables, the pouring of one's hours into the dirt.

At first, I hid from the eccentric graying communards with their big believing eyes. I overheard some of them talking about a willow tree as if it were a person. They seem to move more slowly than the rest of the world and with a degree of care I am unaccustomed to. Most of the commune members never remember me, due to either old age or more pressing spiritual concerns. But I got to know the cooks and carpenters, the mail room, and the herb garden grown into the shape of a pentacle. The commune, like the school up the road, where we keep another field, is housed in old Shaker buildings. So many Believers have already trod upon this same plot of land. As on the other farms, what I feel on Mount Lebanon is the blunt power of nature, nothing more or less.

φ

Sarah grew up in town, born here after her parents met at the commune. I've seen pictures of their wedding on the mountain, the guru's hands held high above her mother's hair, stuck with baby's breath, and her father's red-suspendered shoulders, blessing them both. Her mother was an artist, and her father was a carpenter. Sarah and Ethan took over the farm here after the commune put an ad in the paper seeking farmers since they no longer wanted to run it.

Sarah wrote to me: "I have a proposal, consider moving to NL this winter and getting a job at the diner or the Gallup Inn etc. and make art with me. I know it sounds questionable but I think it could work in some way." The letter closed: "The tie between us is very fine, but a hair never dissolves—Emily Dickinson."

I moved in spring.

Now, we tend twelve acres with two old tractors, one new, and a pair of giant draft horses named Belle and Lou.

Marcella is our fourth farmer. She is short-haired and the best with the little tractors; she lives in an old Shaker house down the farm road and cooks vegetables for us the way her Sicilian grandmother taught her, patiently slicing garlic into thin slivers and simmering greens.

The barn is an ash-colored building that shares a dirt drive with the machine shop and a long wooden shed where we keep our tractors and other supplies dumped and disorganized. Some machines are permanently broken and buried beneath spare parts, while those used daily are more neatly nested in the rubble. The layers of the farm, from this season and many prior, date back to the 1980s, when the people of the commune were young and numerous enough to run it, but the tools themselves date to a much earlier era of farming—horse-drawn manure spreaders and mowers with jagged rust-colored teeth. Still the farm operates within this antiquated realm or spiritual bubble not reflective of the bigness of current-day agriculture. The main farm field is located across a thin creek from the barn and is filled with rounded rocks that do not dissipate under the gentle cultivation of eighty-year-old tractors. We run two identical models distinguishable by one being red, the other once-red.

Across the dirt road from the collective Shaker graveyard, marked by a single stone, the tomato greenhouses share the main field with rows of lettuce, sweet corn, chard, kale, herbs, cucumbers, zucchini, peas, and beans—vegetables kept close and picked often. A chicken coop on wheels is moved incrementally, spreading the poop of sixty birds over our fields after the crops are picked out. The eggs are collected daily and brought to the commune's kitchen, but lately their number has been decreasing. Either the chickens are eating them or the old birds are getting tired.

Apart from the centralized barn, the farm itself is disparate, consisting of piecemeal plots of rented or borrowed land. There's a field surrounded by woods near the end of the road—best loved by deer, who enjoy the cover of the nearby trees, and Sufi neighbors, who, mostly, do not own guns. We grow garlic and potatoes there, things the deer find noxious or at least unappealing. Some years we tempt fate and plant good-tasting cabbage or sweet-leafed cauliflower. A portion of these items are taxed by animals. Away from the barn, toolshed, and maintenance shop the vulnerable plants are not watched over but only found later, sawed down to stalks.

The third field is on the property of the high school, also housed in Shaker buildings. Behind the main buildings, it is little more than a few acres reclaimed from local haymakers who now mow up to the farm fence lines. It is not nestled into Mount

Lebanon but at its breast, so the peaks are visible across the hay-fields. The furthest sight line encompasses the pastures where Belle and Lou graze, so we can see them in their idle hours, and they can see us in nondescript toil. Here we plant salad greens, carrots, beets, cabbages, radishes, rows and rows of green. Unlike the farms in Vermont on riverbank soil, these farms are near no big bodies of water, and for years there was no reliable irrigation, just the luck of weather and timing.

By necessity all three fields are surrounded by tall fences made of electric wire nailed to stripped saplings. These fences, labori-ously set up and maintained, are only partially effective at keeping animals out. Rats, mice, voles, groundhogs, and deer enter above, below, or in between the stinging wires, based on their nature and physiology. Each field, dug up and plowed into productivity from the grass, trees, and wild plants around it, is encircled by a drive path for the tractors, horses, and the truck full of workers that come weekdays during the growing season to plant, cultivate, and extract the bounty.

Sarah, Ethan, Marcella, and I work on a simple fair-weather schedule, Monday through Friday, 7:30 to 5:00. Every Tuesday and Friday afternoon, farm-share members come and pick up vegetables that they paid for in the spring. They'll also fill bags and boxes with pick-your-own flowers, peas, herbs, or toma-toes. The farmers call them "shemmies," a semiderogatory way of turning the customers into a single entity that the vegetables are grown for. If Belle and Lou are not working the fields, they stand in their makeshift stable beside the creek watching the comings and goings under shade. Here they'll rest during the heat of the day, before they are turned out onto pasture to graze under the cool night sky.

The land and the town are old, but the farm, replanted by young workers every year, still feels new.

Before bed one night in June, we eat venison for dinner, big bowls of grilled ribs and chimichurri ground from bouquets of parsley and cilantro. It is a summer deer, illegal to those who respect the sanctioned hunting seasons. Ethan got a special nuisance permit (for hunting) over the phone, but the tags haven't come in the mail yet, so this deer was kind of stealing. Before we cooked it, I swallowed a nearly tasteless, yet succulent, raw piece of loin as the deer was butchered in our backyard.

Marcella grills the ribs. She's got them propped against one another in a kind of corrugated pyramid. We both drink beer and stand by the coals, while she turns and prods the browning meat. Marcella is telling me about how her mother prayed to Saint Jude every day for her father to come home.

"What did Saint Jude do?" I ask.

"He is the saint of lost causes," she says, "and it worked, after two years he [her father] did come home."

When everything is ready, we eat the charred fat and strips of meat pulled from the rib bones, sitting on our porch in the dark of night. The rare summer deer is as sweet as the young cabbages it stole from our fields. Later, we see a fawn without its mother, still eating our cabbage.

That night, I dream of three owls: a screech owl, a barred owl, and a great horned owl. The screech is worse for wear in molting feathers, but perhaps that is just its personality. They are all roosting in the house, recovering from injuries to their wings or talons.

In the same dream there are two deer. The more mature one is hanging from a gambrel, dead. The young one has a rope wrapped around its neck and is still alive. The dreams come unmediated all season long, my mind again and again hitting bluntly at the thin distinction between animation and death.

This season, like every other, I moved for work alone, although I do have a love, an old friend who stayed with me for a month on Gumdrop's farm. A painter, his name is Graham. On his first day with me there, I baked him a big yellow cake for his birthday, one so full of eggs and butter it cost nearly twenty dollars to make. By the last of the month, we were together.

"It only took a 30-pack of Coors Light . . . and three weeks of sleeping together in the same room . . . and almost six years of glances. And conversations. And destroyed memories . . . ," Graham wrote me afterwards.

He lives hours away in New York City, and after a visit this year he writes:

> *It always feels good to be back in NYC even when I'd rather still be in the woods with you . . . I read your letter so many times between today and last night and it got more intense every time to the point where I would look at a single line and have to turn away . . . Coming back to New York and still not having woken up from this grounds it in reality. I'm in a pizza place near Penn Station and I got a Birra Moretti cause that's the beer they have here and I had to borrow a pen and a piece of paper from their printer behind the counter and the beer was $5.44 and the guy flipped the change up in the air before he gave it to me. I love you.*

I love him too, but I am promised to farming, I choose it over him every time. It is not like choosing between two people. How could you trade the sky, the water, or the mountains for a single heart? Instead I imagine the earth opening to take me into its fold. It is beyond personhood. I could be the size of an acorn, moss growing on a tree, or a whole stand of phlox in bloom: a conduit for life to course through. It is an abiding unquantifiable love, but still he and I are promised to one another in other ways. I loved him for years before we were ever together. We would go to the VFW together and sit at the bar, the light of day coming through the windows; it burned to look over into his brown eyes under dark brows. Looking felt like I was already making a vow.

This year, I took Graham to buy some piglets. A nice lady casually mentioned one of her ten children would help load them, each pushing forty pounds, into my truck. I paid in cash. Money she'd spend getting pigs butchered whom she deemed no longer interested in the business of being mothers. Graham stood on her farm and watched the rats, children, and animals, his sneakers drowning in manure, before lifting the screaming piglets out of the pen, away from their mother, and dropping them into an old dog crate in my truck's bed. The woman sent us home with homemade bagels wrapped in a paper towel and frozen hot dogs.

I moved the pigs into a scrubby patch of trees on the next-door neighbor's property, a ten-minute walk from our yellow house. These pigs are not part of any of my farm jobs but uphold a simpler custom that Ethan, Sarah, and I recognize to stock our freezer for winter.

The New Lebanon Sunday flea market is held off Route 20 on the former grounds of the nation's first pharmaceutical company. A next-door neighbor dug up spadefuls of medicine bottles in his garden. He found even more, by the blue glittering hundred, in his pond during a drought. Though evidence like that remains, before industry ever really hit big here, the town fell back into rurality. The once commonplace dairy farms are now no more than hayfields. Instead of things being built up, they wore away. Or burnt down and turned to ash.

The big man selling CDs on the grassy lawn of the former

bottling plant talks to me while I try to read the words on oppos-ing jewel cases he has crammed into cardboard boxes: Brenda Lee, *Led Zeppelin III*. "You got any Jimmy Buffett?" someone asks.

The salesman, casting shadows on his merchandise from a shirt like a Hawaiian-print sail, tells me he keeps a German shepherd.

"I have a twenty-pound yellow cat," he says, "an' a Maine coon with the most beautiful face."

"Me too!" I say appreciatively, picturing Goose at the edge of the forsythia bush we've let grow across the width of our lawn. It is there he brings his dead, decapitated finches-mice-snakes-rabbits, into the obscurity of its branches.

The CD seller has seen friends, loved ones die, but he can't bear it that his "sweet" German shepherd is nine now, knowing as a habitual pet owner that she isn't too long for this world.

"I work on a pig farm and I've got my own pigs at home," I offer, not knowing what to say for the shepherd.

"Oh! Pigs are great," he says, really meaning it. We easily bal-ance the conversation between cuts of meat and the virtues of swine personalities.

I hold up the *Super Fly* soundtrack. "I love this one."

"That's a good one. Have you seen *Used Cars* with Kurt Rus-sell?" he asks.

"No."

"Oh, you're sheltered!" he says.

He asks if I know about a cable channel that plays tractor pulls and draft horse competitions. "I don't have a TV," I say, more apologetically this time.

That night, I go to bed at 3:00 a.m. By 7:00 a.m. my piglets have escaped. Sarah had heard them calling for me in the front lawn and thinks we're psychically connected, me and the pigs.

In early sunlight, I carry an orange bucket of feed down the driveway. A neighbor across the road says he saw the pigs moving through his lawn. I walk down the road, past the big forsythia bush and the pond, to the fields interrupted by homes. In the warm and quiet morning, I do not see any flashes of swine body on the neighbor's property. I ring the doorbell. A woman with a gray bob opens the front door, exposing a breezy modern interior—heavy spiked light fixtures and shampooed carpets, expansive paintings and impractical picture windows that probably get covered in ice during the winter. Weekenders. "I saw the pigs go that way," she says, pointing around the back corner of the house. She held sliced fruit out in her hand for them, but they didn't stop for her. She's met them before, she says.

I circle behind the house. There's a cement statue of a head sinking into the lawn with meadows flowing behind it. I start to follow the perpendicular paths of tire tracks across open fields swollen with mud.

I find pig tracks stuck deep in the mud, seeing them first as inverted deer tracks before I turn and get oriented to their direction. Thorns make runs on my legs as if they were cheap fabric. I stop at a swamp. The pigs walked around the cattails on supple ground. No evidence of foraging (like miniature explosions in the dirt). They just took the old logging roads, enjoying the moving air against the cool mud coats they acquired along the way. Everywhere bedstraw blooms in tiny white clusters that choke the field grass. The air is heavy with the smell of its nectar.

I start to wonder if they're really gone. Worry they are circling an irate farmer tedding hay with spinning implements and driving unrelentingly forward or eating out of a poisonous rhubarb patch in someone's vegetable garden. Or worse yet, in the sights of the hunters down the road who make garish gun blasts all weekend behind their house.

I named the two littermates Brother Sun and Sister Moon, after the movie about Saint Francis. In time, Sister Moon will take the shape of a stately claw-foot tub, her blond spotted body curving elegantly around her haunches, which end in four flesh-colored hooves. Brother Sun will more closely resemble a stove-pipe, flaming red and stubbornly round. He'll sometimes bite people who don't know how to comport themselves around pigs. But for now, the pigs are small. When they first came to me, their ears barely crested the green in the wooded pasture—I could find them by those points and the sound of roughage passing through their snouts. When I visit them after work, they'll sniff my hand, which holds a can of Hamm's, and they will drink the beer if I pour it out into the dirt for them. Their low-set eyes look down into a world brown and wet and swirled with beer or leaves. First Sister will let me scratch her, then Brother too.

Finally, I find them, shaggy red and blond cutouts against the grass. When they see me, they greet me as an old friend, seesawing their fixed rectangular bodies toward me, ears flapping in happy abandon. We walk pleasantly the mile or so out together, with me sometimes leading or one of them heading the procession with purpose. They really are perfect company, I think. No word need be exchanged, just spending time. We cross the road and leave behind the statue of the head. Sometimes one pig will speed up and accidentally push their nose into my calf, a cool lily pad.

I fence in a new corner of the woods for them. The first thing they make is an elliptical dirt clearing to sleep in. Not mud, but loam, and I realize I'm late to get to Henry and Alice's for my shift there.

I work in steel-toed boots, pointed so that I look like a witch but also a construction worker. My best T-shirt is one Sarah bought me, extra-large and pink, covered in a pig face so blown out its black eyes rest at my armpits, its snout on my belly button. I look young because of my thin body, but with sun wrinkles coming in. I wear my long hair piled beneath a baseball cap and on days when it rains, oversized rubber coveralls that swish when I walk. It is skilled work, but it's not good money. Besides a fondness for the days, I like the concrete task of producing food, and my hands are trained by years of repetition at bunching radishes, trellising tomatoes, setting up fences.

Part of the job is losing oneself in nature. Cast out into the farm amongst the plants, animals, machines, I feel unindividuated. Of course, I act upon the world. But the work is so elemental as to be impersonal: animals fed, dirt plowed. The weather acts; I accept. If I leave, another will surely take my place. I see a sign at Price Chopper that says they're hiring at sixteen dollars per hour in the deli—more than any of my farm jobs pay—but those who *choose* to farmhand (and many don't get the luxury of choice without papers or a clean record or the ability to pass a drug test) have good reason: a freedom that goes beyond working for someone else, just as answerable to weather or bugs. It is never my farm to run, anyway. The seasonal work is a kind of stasis happening year after year. There is no ending and no beginning to an agricultural story, only a descent into a repeating cycle.

It is not necessarily so impersonal to work as a farmhand, but I feel like a different kind of person, a person addressed to plants, animals, or machines. Often my thoughts with the plants are dumb. I think of the weeds I am pulling or count what I am picking. Animals, like Alice and Henry's tank-shaped sows, I can read better in a mammalian sense. Touch them, watch how they behave, see when they back away or come forward, hear when they call out. There is no embarrassment in watching and one needn't ask, but farm animals are different from the wild ones, who may choose to stay hidden. There is so much else to understand besides the clogged world of human activity. But on the farm, I carry out unkind human intentions or make ugly mistakes. Geese, fattening nicely for Christmastime, accidentally hang themselves in the cross wire of a fence I set up. I removed their downy bodies, so close to slaughtering size, and fed them to the dog. I pruned tomatoes for more fruit, but instead spread a brown wasting disease so that as they fruited they rotted. I plowed with the tractor over sod-covered earth and turned it from living soil to blowing dust. After years of this work I still falter, spoiling the life we are cultivating.

A farm itself is a system that is always somewhat out of control. An order imperfectly blanketing wildness. But there is still pride to be had in a well-run farm. The task is in getting a living thing to flourish, corralling life toward the desired fecundity. This aliveness is not a human achievement, but simply a condition of nature. We pride ourselves on our manipulations, but it cannot go beyond that. In the fostering of this raw thing—life—lies the reward.

Without understanding life, one can farm. It is a profession based on so much work already done, the earth tricked so many centuries ago. The cooperation of plants and animals remains a mystery to my stubbornly unscientific mind. I am taught to plant potatoes on Good Friday, to tap trees for sap when the days are warm and the nights freezing, to guide a pig into a trailer with its ear and tail as rudders, to look for the yellow spot that indicates a ripe melon. I read on the bag what ratio of bonemeal to spread for fertilizer. There is an equation to weigh a pig without a scale: square the girth of the animal, multiply by length, and divide by 400. The whole thing feels predestined and the formulas predetermined in these carefully laid plans. Now what is left, each year renewed, is the work.

There is the established wisdom, but still there are no false promises. Things thrive or die, and the farmer hopes to tip the balance toward bounty. Most years it is okay. But I've seen the cruel waters of flood eat away at a field or the cracked soil of no rain or worms rot a flock of sheep from the hooves up. Enough to know that life remains wild. For this reason too I like farming: one simply must accept the outcome. Here one's hard work becomes like a prayer instead of a stubborn insistence that things will turn out okay. The work exists in a moment of suspension.

II

Mating

Early Summer 2017, New Lebanon, NY

At Alice and Henry's farm, it is time to mate the sows. Henry even bought a home pregnancy test for them—it is inserted into the vagina and simply beeps, with maddeningly little explanation, if it judges them to have conceived. It is 50 percent accurate, he says. At six foot four, Henry walks the fence with his feet turned out looking for his two sister sows in their brush-filled pen. Tied around his head he wears a bandanna, which quickly darkens with his sweat. I work between Henry and Alice, helping one while the other takes care of the baby.

Henry borrows a red boar of strange constitution from a friend and unloads it from a horse trailer into the sows' pen. The boar's eyes are too close together and brightly green instead of the humane shade of gray I've come to expect from pigs. He's hardly the stock you want to multiply, but the sister sows are of what might be unshakable genetics, entirely stubborn animals. Both are black, around seven hundred pounds, and slow to follow all commands. When grain is poured into their pen, they gather it at the front of their mouths and tilt their heads back in violent shakes, all the better to funnel the feed directly to their stomachs before fighting over the scraps.

The boar, about four hundred pounds lighter than his mates, follows the sows. They tolerate him sniffing their vulvas while they forage for food, but eventually they turn, looking over their broad backs to bite him hard on the neck, sending him in a shamed loop that ends again at the points of their vulvas. Otherwise, he moves further from their warm bodies toward their fresh urine in the grass, which he smells and often seems to determine "not ovulating" before momentarily giving up and ambling into the shade.

When one of the sows does lend herself to the boar's advances, she stands still, an unmoving slate rectangle. He climbs up behind her and inserts his curling penis, nudging it along. She allows this with a nonchalant grace. Only one sister at a time lets him hang around her.

On the opposite side of their wire fence, ten uncastrated males are enraptured, studying the act upon which their agricultural survival depends, but of course they don't know this. While the procreative sex is happening, they play at mounting one another, and other boars sit, as dogs, and respectfully watch. Some carry streaks of white smeared onto their hams, the semen of other juvenile boars practicing at sex.

Alice brings out the baby in his stroller after lunch. I don't know if his eyes can see far enough to make out what's happening or if he can only inspect the clover around the wheels of the stroller. And there's his mother's shape to monitor as she moves through the field setting up fresh pasture for the pigs. His gaze follows her almost everywhere.

The two farm dogs are also here with the baby and his parents, the pigs, and me. They ate a robin I tried to rescue from drowning and also, I think, the killdeers' ground nest I found hidden in wild thyme. They find everything little and kill it and their breath is terrible. Alice dries pig liver for them and keeps it shriveled inside a treat jar. The dogs like me and bark at me like crazy. I let them rest on the cool heads of lettuce in the field even though it kills some of the plants.

When his mother is gone from his sight, the baby will smile at me and the pigs, consent to be touched, and the farm truck will finally slip into reverse out of the fecund field and back toward the disarrayed driveway and white farmhouse. I always look for the baby when I back up. A cousin of mine in Vermont has a toddler who got hit by a mower. I sent her daisies in the hospital. She will be able to go home in a month, we *hope*. They have to get the grass out of her stomach and piece back together the bones of her foot and her hand. Her dad jokes that he should throw holy water on her mother, who was *supposed* to be watching her, to see if she gets burned. My stepmom called to tell me about the accident while I was at the farm, but I didn't say anything to Alice and Henry because I didn't want to jinx their baby. Instead I went home and cried on my front porch over the bad things that can happen to innocent creatures.

Some days, Ben, the cook from the Sufi commune, gives me old food to feed Brother and Sister. The Sufis don't eat pork, but the cook is my friend. He has a buzz cut and cheeks flushed pink from the big ovens. He is young like me and self-effacing about his cooking. He laughs when he tells me he has to make salmon for a wedding party and thinks he'll do a bad job. He lives at the end of the farm road with Marcella and his black-and-white pit bull, which looks like it is wearing a tuxedo. He unclogged the toilet at the gas station once, so now they give him free coffee. Another time, he showed me a wool sweater he found bunched up in the septic tank at the commune, a much worse clog.

Today, he gives me milk crates full of half-and-half. He directs a few workers in the open kitchen, then points me to the basement, where on top of the unrefrigerated milk crates he's left a scrap of paper that says $\mathcal{Pig}$. I decide to pour out the containers of half-and-half before I get to the pigs' pen so I don't have to hear the pigs' anticipatory screams for food, but I wonder if they can hear me all the way from the road unscrewing the milk and glug-glugging it into buckets. I drink some first; it's still good, and this time of year I'm so hungry. When the pigs' portion is poured out, they lower their heads luxuriously into the white bowl of milk and suck in long powerful breaths of it. They fight and spill some of the milk, and then they roll in the puddle, cooling off from the day. It looks like a crater on the moon, gray and murky.

They are getting fatter every day and they carry the weight well, muscling out their shoulders and lengthening their stomachs into long strips of bacon. There is a tradition to this, the family pig—a "mortgage lifter"—an animal that judiciously eats the kitchen scraps and is converted back to food for the same table, the excesses of which can be sold as the cold comes.

Brother and Sister like touching me when I'm in their pen, even though it is often to get at their food. They have never been gentle with their own bodies, but they press their noses pleasantly against my bare thigh or the soft corduroy fabric of my pants. They sit on the toes of my boots, squishing the rubber against their rounded hindquarters.

They are archaeologists, showing me the old farm, which is reforested now, as they force their snouts through the undergrowth. Over time, skeins of barbed wire appear, beer cans with antique fasteners, iron parts of tractors, a contractor bag (which they shredded like mice making a nest), an apple peeler, paint cans, milk pails, mushrooms from ancient spores. Their pen has begun to stink. The smell comes from their wallow and digested food. They leave uneaten fruit and vegetable rinds shriveled in the dirt and pushed out of their fence to rot.

I find witches' butter, a strange and luminescent orange fungus hanging improbably from a stick, in a corner encroaching on their bathroom. It is slick like plastic, almost tacky, and yet delicately puffed into three-dimensionality like a paper lantern. It is attached to the stick by a thin stalk, as oysters do with one foot clinging through the tides in their tough shells. I take the stick home and display it on our kitchen table—it looks just as beautiful as the magnified pictures in the field guide.

Aside from Alice, I am friends with three or four women with kids in town. One is a potter and her front porch is full of lumpy things she's made. She has twin boys and survived cancer when she was carrying them. They have an older sister, a beautiful nine-year-old, named Eva. Eva does things like paint every morning while wearing a kimono. I thought I was done babysitting by the time I was seventeen, but my car needs a new windshield, so I agree to babysit the twins and Eva. When I arrive at their house the twins are dressed in matching sailor shirts, but otherwise naked.

"The boys are fighting over one Playmobil man," their father says. "If it gets to be a problem, fry it in some butter."

Their mom lets Eva dress her for their date, and she is wearing gemstone jewelry and a long skirt.

After their parents leave, I make us a spaghetti and jam-bread picnic, which we eat in the backyard. Eva, who has a handsome near unibrow, is losing her baby teeth and reading *King Arthur*. When the twins talk, they say, "yeah, us know them," instead of "we." After they've lost interest in the food and scraped the sweet jam from the bread, they make up words and chant them while flailing on the tire swing.

They are supposed to take a bath before bed, but first Eva offers to teach me how to play chess. The four of us crowd into the bathroom and Eva mists everyone with lavender perfume. The twins zoom a toy motorboat around in the tub while Eva, skipping the bath, stands in front of the mirror hiking up her shorts and prances around the bathroom. I wash her hair in the sink like at a beauty parlor, then pull the stopper out of the boys' bathtub without asking if they're done.

Their shared bedroom has three oversized beds and overflowing dressers. We read a Richard Scarry book full of animals in cars, a book about an ape, and one about a wise man. When I leave them to sleep, one of the twins falls off the bed and smacks the back of his big head on the ground. "Check his eyes, we always check his eyes first!" Eva wails while I try to make sure, in the darkness, that he is wet from tears instead of blood. He looks at me blankly, screaming. When I turn the light on his siblings turn their backs to him and read a picture book. I lie in the big soft bed with them until we all fall asleep.

Their parents send me home with a grocery bag of chicken of the woods mushrooms, orange and smelling like schmaltz, as well as sixty dollars.

At home in my own bed beneath the slanting floral-wallpapered ceiling of the yellow house, I talk on the phone with Graham. Lying in darkness, I tell him I want kids now. Really, I don't want to be old, I want to be young and healthy like the plants of the field or even the swollen sows. The pressure of this makes him so upset he cries. He thinks of youth as meant for something else, not to be used in the service of child rearing; it scares him, this kind of talk. My aunt told me once in a dark theater, before the movie started, that she had a two-year-old at my age. The phone conversation ends with prolonged silence filled with the weight of static on both ends.

There is my deep and mysterious longing for a child, and then there is the problem that I am promised to the farm. But still, I want a baby with him. I find myself yearning for the sweetness of children, their small personhood and imaginations, and their accompaniment through life. I assign them the same unknowing goodness as I do the animals. I know that they can be terrible like the rest of us, but I see them from far off like lambs of the field: a child in tow at Family Dollar, another fed onion rings at the fair, taken to the speedway and flanked by relations, or sat down to read at the library, a sweater pulled tight over a young girl's head so that her hair forms a wild halo of static.

III

Springs

Summer 2017, New Lebanon, NY

On this, as every morning, Brother and Sister are brought food and water, which they require in increasing amounts as their bodies round and their thirst grows. The pen loses green with mounting rapidity until I move them to fresh pasture—new squares of wood for them to mow down and turn over. One of the first marks of the pigs is that all the raspberry canes have been bowed with their newly grown tips pressed forcibly back into the ground. After stomping down the thorn-covered canes, they eat the leaves and the plants are left bare.

On our afternoon off, Sarah and I take a walk across town, past planted feed corn, trailers, Victorian houses, and the town hall, to drink from the Lebanon spring. We walk through the cultivated valley scavenged by Canada geese and up a steep hill. There used to be a hotel here and a bath with the circumference of a silo. Bathers would come from all over to enjoy the spring's waters. Everything here grows special. The water stays seventy-one degrees all year round. When tasted it is warm to the lips, not stagnant but amenable to the temperature of the body and the blood. In our time, part of the Lebanon spring has been redirected into a black hose. To drink from it without sinking into the puddle beneath, which is ringed in vibrant green chickweed, Sarah has to stand with her legs spread wide.

BLESSED WATER, WINE OF THE GODS is carved on the rock that once provided a statelier fountain. The abandonment of pretense at the spring echoes through the rest of New Lebanon. Sarah says there used to be a bar here that looked just like a ship, but it burnt down a long time ago.

We sit on my shirt, spread beneath a sycamore tree that grows straight from the spring. It is so big I did not see it the first time I came here. From under the tree we can still hear the hose flowing, but it is hidden now behind the hexagonal bathhouse built beneath the sycamore. Bulbous mounds press out from the tree's limbs, "like souls got caught in the tree," Sarah says. The once merry bathers? Or did the whole town get fenced in by some fairy ring?

The tree's giant trunk splits into three, each still bigger around than a normal tree, which explode into further trunks and open-palmed green leaves. In the sunlight, the bark is white as milk. Now it is the color of sand and concrete. The tree's missing branch has grown, over time, into a completely smooth knob.

In 1857, Benson John Lossing visited and tasted the spring, like "rain-water-soft and sweet," on his way to meet the Mount Lebanon Shakers. A century and a half ago he saw the "magnificent Sycamore, full ten feet in circumference at its base, which was planted there by the original proprietor of the spring, after it had been used by him as a riding-slip for a whole day."

"I wonder if this tree has ever had any diseases?" Sarah asks.

"How would we be able to tell?" I say.

"Well, maybe this tree can't have diseases 'cause it grows over the spring," she says. Sarah easily sleeps with her head on my shoulder, like an animal, when we ride in the work truck or at the movie theater, something I would never do. She's more fanciful than I am and more beautiful too, with fierce blue eyes and dark lashes, but we both see the good in nature.

The shuttered bathhouse is topped with a white spire, pointing a bony finger at the otherworldly tree. There is a piece missing from the bark whose shape looks like the rabbit in the moon. One branch has a scar from growing too fast, and it is twisted like a muscle or a snake in water.

Every time we come here, we peer into the bathhouse windows. The structure encloses a rotted basin with PVC piping arching over it. Pallets and netting—supplies for something great—are stored beside it. It is a place for nymphs. A place where the Mohican tribe brought sick settlers before they were betrayed by them. Some families still live here because an incurable relative came to be healed.

Stone eagles turn their heads and look away from the abandoned fountain. Urns are now pregnant with weeds. Another cast-iron fountain lined with swans, necks drooped gracefully against their chests, is also dry now. The rock memorializing the spring has been washed smooth, slowly erasing each letter carved into it. The spring has its own self-made viriditas, unstitching the seams of the bathhouse and the stone replicas of birds and prayers and the finery necessary to public parks and European gardens, a pretense that never quite fit here.

The Gallup Inn, the other kind of watering hole, and one that Sarah also used to lure me here, closes early even on the weekends, but we go there after the springs anyway. Last call is around ten, depending on the night. The regulars are old. The sign is made of plastic, the black silhouette of a horse lit up so that it shines at night. It is an after-work bar and a bar for people done with work altogether, or contractors with irregular hours who sometimes arrive by three in the afternoon. A habitual scan of the dirt lot that surrounds the squat building, and reaches on various sides to the town dump, Route 22, and the bank, reveals whose car is there like a totem for the person inside. Because it is an offtrack betting bar, the TVs, little and old-fashioned, are tuned to horse races whenever they are on. A little machine in the corner is used for placing bets, but it is at least a thirty-minute drive to redeem a winning ticket.

The bar itself stands on one end of the room, a wooden U with three taps. The bartender floats in her narrow lane, her purse wilted on the countertop beside the register before bags of chips, T-shirts with horses on them, and shelves of cheap liquor hung from the wall. All the bartenders here are women, each with her own night of the week; ranging from grandmotherly to motherly, they run the bar with an air of casual intimacy.

Tonight, the bleached-blond bartender, skewing more toward grandmotherly, wears a pink tie-dyed Saratoga Race Course shirt with the races playing behind her. She hoists a gallon of unrefrigerated milk onto the bar and says, "Don't you have pigs or something?"

"Yeah, they'll love this," I say.

"That's how you get them fat," someone at the bar adds.

People hang around outside smoking cigarettes and eating the awful hot dogs they serve. It stinks of the nearby cow pastures in waves between beer and cigarettes, but all that is visible is the parking lot and the dump under the darkening sky. The building manager, who has been repainting the outside of the bar, sucks in on a cigarette. His cheeks deflate, retracting from his sunburnt and dazed face. He is also wearing a tie-dyed shirt but instead of horses his has chickens on it. He says he's been feeding the same crow every day while painting and every day it comes to visit him. One day it came with a gold ring in its beak.

"So it proposed to you?" I ask.

"Yes."

"Did you say yes?"

"Yes. Now I'm married to a crow."

That night, Graham arrives at the yellow house. In the morning, we wake to find a black bear in the yard. Its first distinguishable characteristics: rounded ears and the way its soft fur sticks out against the texture of serrated grass around it. It possesses a kind of benevolent calm, crossing the lawn in a slow diagonal, placing down one foot, then the other. It walks through thorn bushes unfazed and back into the woods, all at an even clip. A good omen.

Graham has come to drive to Vermont with me. My step-grandma Joan died. She was my stepmom's (my mother's wife's) mother. Before she retired she worked at the microchip factory in town and drove a truck for a clothing company. She had me over to her house around Christmastime to see the Christmas village she set up, saying one day I could have part of it. She was really proud of me for going to school and always sent me cards with money even though I knew she didn't have a lot.

When I try to write, the most familiar things become erased, the people I love most even. I can see some pieces of nature better—the animals, the growing plants—without the chaos of talk, which I also forget without my notebook. Strangers' faces appear as if under a magnifying glass, the beloved from a lens smeared in Vaseline. They are too big to see or else simply seeing them betrays the thing itself.

My family likes when I bring Graham home. His buzz cut has grown out this summer, light brown and soft as a child's. He wears his old Nikes and black pants with paint on them. My aunt tells him if we get married, she'll sew him a Christmas stocking with his name on it. Before Joan died, she said to Graham, forcefully, "She's a good woman!" pointing at my chest, either hoping to make him stick around or else threatening him to treat me right.

The service is held in the afternoon at a Victorian funeral parlor next door to where I grew up. At the funeral parlor, flowers are set up around Joan's ashes, which are in a little box on an altar draped in red velvet. There are flowers from her grandkids, my mom's dog (who sent a bouquet with a paw-print sash), and the couple who owns the Vietnamese restaurant in town. Two women who were variously Joan's lovers sent a large bunch with BFF written on the ribbon holding the stems together. There is no talk of God during the service. Joan's partner, Connie, is here, her ex-husband, and her friends too. There are photo albums with pictures of her playing basketball and dancing.

People stand up and tell stories about Joan. A guy my step-mom, Linda, worked with installing HVAC tells a story of coming over to help Joan put in a washing machine; he found her at home to be just like her daughter. There are old butch women with pompadours and military haircuts in freshly washed jeans. The witch I used to house-sit for is here too. She has a garden of garlic and a cat with no eyes who can still catch mice. And my old babysitter who let me sit and watch her at the vanity putting fresh hairspray on her bangs. My sister stands next to me during the service. Somebody sings "Amazing Grace" in the quiet parlor.

After the memorial we all go to my mother's, a house I returned to often for Sunday dinner when I still lived nearby, for a buffet. Graham is quiet, respectfully looming over the mourners and biting into a chocolate cupcake, while my cousin whose daughter got run over by the mower tells me how she's doing, what his daughter will have left for a foot, how scarred up her hand is, and the different ages at which she'll need more surgeries.

My great-aunt, sitting in the kitchen and eating a vanilla funeral cupcake, tells me the most real thing that ever happened to her was when her father died and he communicated "something vast" to her. Those few minutes of her life were bigger than almost anything else she's experienced. Also, she almost drowned when she was seven, and she was not afraid to die.

The only person who seems to be missing is Joan. All her family, her nieces, grandchildren, and great-grandchildren, are here. Up until now, she's held them all together. I was not there with them when she died and for months after, dumbly, I doubt the reality of it. Her death was perhaps simply exacted for a life lived.

Before Joan died I saw her at her granddaughter's baby shower. Her kid came when she was relatively young, the pregnancy came easily. With a little oxygen tank wheeled by her side, Joan told me, "Everyone's looking at me like I'm already dead!" The shower was held on the second floor of the local VFW hall so that the men could drink downstairs. The upstairs was decorated with giant baby bottles made of balloons and there were watermelons carved into bassinets with little cantaloupe babies in them and a sheet cake decorated in fluffy feminine roses. The mom to be, with her swollen belly, sat on a throne covered in pink muslin blooming out around her like the petals of an opening flower.

Graham and I cross back into New York by nightfall, and a wild storm surrounds the yellow house. Under the porch lights, what looks like a red dog stands huffing in the downpour at 10:00 p.m. When the purple lightning flashes, his silhouette darkens against

the sky and I can make out the creases in fat jowls and the cylindrical wattles of a pig. I could have sworn, in the light, Brother's
eyes turned green, just like those of the boar at the farm. His sister
appears on the lawn, in a pink flash of her bathtub-shaped body.

It is easy to follow the white line of the road back to the field
where they live. The grass is silver this time of night. But the
woods are harder to see through. I walk in front, followed by two
pigs, Graham, and more houseguests, one with no shoes, excited
at the novelty of it. The rain is falling so hard it pools around
the lower lids of our eyes before falling again as tears and filling
the furrows between top and bottom lips. We are all falling into
puddles, tripping over large stumps of quartz and barbed wire
stretched between trees.

When we get to the pigs' pen, the flimsy fence is splayed like
a rib cage, white wire and posts sticking out at terrible angles. I
dump more food to keep the pigs inside the mess, while trying
to tighten wire, sink poles back into the ground, and straighten
the fence out again. We leave them there, but I do not know if
they'll be home when I come back.

In the morning, Goose is on the roof. I can see him from the
soap-stained window pointing out of the shower. I think it is not
a cat on the roof traveling in feline symmetry but a further larger
pig on the lawn. We make eye contact, though, as if to reassure
each other of our existence.

IV

Brother Sun, Sister Moon

Late Summer 2017, New Lebanon, NY

August arrives with a thick heat. The plants on Ethan and Sarah's farm grow fast in heavy sunshine. It is time to mow the vegetable fields before everything goes to seed—the bluish rye grass and bolted crops alike trying to spread newer generations, too much green. The mower is a flat semicircle towed behind the tractor. When the mower crashes on, the blade beneath its metal housing gets to its hidden beheading. I drive forward and look back over the seat of the tractor at the shorn field. The ground takes on a lighter shade of green. The freshly torn stalks are soon matted with a cud of plants. Rocks circulate heavily against the mower blade and the metal machine catches on the ground, digging brown sickle-shaped dents in the land.

I move from crops onto open field, wild grasses mixed with clover and poison ivy. It smells sweet, the incense of running motors and hay. The metal seat is hot beneath me and I bounce obediently with the tractor. Sun hits the tops of my thighs and working pipes press metallic breath against my skin. I drive standing up to see above the tide of green with both hands draped over the thin steering wheel. Rabbits begin to run in terror at wild angles away from the wheels, dusty brown spirits. It is easy, visual work. The tractor is in gear and I don't change speed. Birds have made their nests in the ground. Some hop away, one wing splayed out as if in a splint. Are they faking it like the killdeers? Even butterflies are flung about as the dog-nosed tractor parses the grass. I make patterns mowed in stripes or triangles around rocks.

Lydia, a beef farmer in town, leaves whole swaths of milkweed unmowed for the monarchs to feed on. The other hay farmers make fun of her for it, but she doesn't care. She welcomes the muskrat to her pond too. She can decipher him all the way from the cow yard by a simple V carved out on the water's surface trailing behind the slick point of his head. She decided to become a beef farmer as a child when she saw an oil painting of cows, because of how beautiful they were. Her cows have dappled coats like granite; a whole generation of them are named after flowers. The new calves all have white bodies with black noses and ears. She lives alone with the cows.

I watch the other women in town—the mothers, the farmers, the ones dedicated to animals—and imagine the different kinds of people I could become with the right training. I interviewed Lydia, the cattle farmer, and Rickie, a reptile keeper, for the local newspaper, thinking their dedication to be newsworthy in and of itself; I wanted to see into their worlds, the way Lydia watches over her calves and Rickie organizes her snakes in drawers. Long after I wrote the articles, I continue to look at the pictures I took: Rickie with a snake wrapped around her strong forearm, its head held lightly in her palm, her eyes cast down in total regard; Lydia facing a cow and a group of calves, speaking to them. She told me in all seriousness, the cows "are not unlike humans, they're typically better than humans." Ethan told me he thinks of Belle and Lou as toddlers, that he sees most animals as children of some kind, especially for some reason our huge draft horses.

Rickie keeps a ranch house full of reptiles off a dirt road near the yellow house. Outside, there are Dalmatians and cats, a husband and a cockatiel. Inside is dense with cages of tarantulas, snakes in every color, geckos, and fat iguanas, two freezers full of rodents to feed them all. In the basement turtles and a tank full of real alligators. Snakes can hold sperm until conditions are right when the females want to get pregnant, but sometimes they become egg bound and die. The alligators are the only reptiles she keeps that have any kind of true maternal instinct, who'll look after their young for a couple years. She hangs posters all over town advertising that she'll bring reptiles to parties, though she's not allowed to cross state lines with certain snakes. There are big fines for that. She brings them in boxes so no one can see what's inside until she pulls out the animal. People like to be surprised. She pulls extra shifts at the diner to support them all. Once, she found an alligator tooth lodged in her arm, but she doesn't know how it got there. Snakes bite mostly because they can't see well; to get them out you have to relax them first because their teeth are backwards.

When I am at work on Alice and Henry's pig farm, my hidden lunch spot is underneath two maple trees that, from above, look like one. In the shade there's an upside-down bucket to use as a table. My lunch is laid out on it: venison shepherd's pie inside a yogurt container and a mug full of water from the spigot. When I finish eating I will clean the cucumbers and squash I left floating in bins of water and then pick rattlesnake beans, the ripe ones with purple veins.

Henry is inside making a pinhole camera because today is the eclipse. When he comes out he is carrying a long lens on a stand, white paper, and masking tape. I wonder if the baby, now eight months old and seeming adult, will watch too. I've known him three months now. His hair has turned orange and his teeth have grown in long and white; I know because he smiled at me. He has a unibrow now, equally faint from end to end. He can say "Ma Ma Ma" in syncopated rhythm. He's even tried barbecue. They say babies really do like meat. He is sitting in his stroller and clutching his mother's sweaty hat while she works, enjoying her scent, which is also his own. At work Alice is surprisingly strong, moving with unselfconscious severity, fitting metal poles together or forking up sod while the baby cries from the stroller. I found an old studio photograph of her in an unfinished room of the farmhouse that betrays her grace. Her thin neck and delicate features against an absent white background, the sideways look of her green-glass-colored eyes.

Later, Henry, Alice, and I watch a piece of paper held beneath the camera lens. Henry holds the paper steady and we take turns looking through the thick lens. At first only the paper appears, but then it is punctuated by celestial movement: white disk of light, the sun's external gases, the membranes of the clouds, and the dark disk of moon are all illuminated in an oddly transparent tableau that wavers across the page and again is gone when the clouds become too thick.

The crickets grow loud and the sky dims a few shades bluer. The pigs sleep through all of it and the plants respire.

Alice brings the baby indoors and my work continues.

Henry backs the trailer into the field adjacent to the wood-lot, where the boar has been trying, with much uncertainty, to impregnate the sister sows. Now all we can do is hope. Henry opens the fence with obvious escape routes in the hope the boar will intuitively enter its new pen or follow his lead. But there's the green of the surrounding fields to distract him, if he doesn't spook first.

Some pigs are too young, not yet acclimated to following commands, and the sows remember bitterly slipping off the trailer or the sting of the electric fence. Even though they are seven hundred pounds, I have seen them reduced to quivering masses at the thought of venturing out of their pen. Once when we tried to move the sows from the field to the woods, they got so nervous they began hyperventilating in the midday sun and had to be doused with water underneath a shade canopy jerry-rigged of stakes with a tarp tied between them. But, their hearts kept pumping blood like hoses and they were only nervy.

When the boar, who has outworn his welcome in price of feed, is scheduled to be sent home, it is another uncertain maneuver. I lay out new ElectroNet fence in long white ribbons before pushing the posts into the ground with all my weight to create a passageway to the trailer. We make piles of grain in the pen, but they, by some logic, attract only the sows, and then we bait the boar with a bucket of corn, peas, and whey, capping the tip of his snout. He hesitates as we cross the threshold. Some animals can decipher the timed clicks of a power fence. Because of the slop, the boar consents to leaving his pen and going into the new one constructed around the horse trailer that will take him home. The boar is doing it. He walks up the ramp, but we don't act quick enough. The door hangs open and he walks out again.

If the load doesn't happen right away anxiety starts to set in instead of the pigs thinking that they are on a walk that ends in a paradisiacal bowl of cream on soft hay. Now the boar follows the bucket only haphazardly, looking with one eye at the fresh forage. He doesn't like the gap between the ramp and the trailer, which emits an inch of disorienting light. He doesn't like the way the light seems sucked out of the long metal tube he's supposed to walk into. Henry half runs after the boar, sweating into his bandanna and jiggling the rubber bucket of feed. He dumps feed on the grass, which only deters the boar further from wanting to enter the trailer. A pig, with its oversized mouth, will parse out meal from between individual blades of grass, delicately working its tongue and lower jaw for as long as it takes.

The last pig farmer I worked for—Gumdrop the unexpectant sow's owner—was quiet, a grown man who blushed. When he was trying to load pigs on a trailer I saw him, with all his might, thrust his body against the back end of a pig over and over, which did not work. Sometimes, with animals, you start to lose your mind. Eventually, he constructed a large ring out of woven wire, which he covered in an old sheet so the pigs couldn't see through, and used it as a lasso. He would hurl the ring over a pig or a squirming pack of piglets. Grown pigs were only momentarily trapped before they forced up the bottom of the wire with their noses, bending it enough to wriggle their fat bodies out from under it.

"Sometimes I think I'm going to hell," he said once. "What do you think of raising animals for profit?" he asked me.

"They have to come from somewhere," I replied. We had already eaten pork chops together by then, easily and with quick hunger, another shared intimacy with the pigs.

Eventually, I get the boar eating, face deep into the bucket so that his eyes see the perimeter of the bucket's rubber edge and little else. After shaking me off he changes his mind and reenters the bucket world. This time we travel, me with the bucket by my hip, motored along by his prodding, up the ramp and into the back of the trailer. Henry quickly shuts the back door and again I find myself in a black trailer with a pig. I watch the boar sniff abjectly in the dark while Henry opens the side door in a flash of sunlight, and I slip out before the boar notices. Some pigs get angry in enclosures, others go into a near-comatose sleep, waiting.

ϕ

The next morning on my habitually made grass path through a hayfield from our yellow house to Brother and Sister, I scream from startling a flock of twenty turkeys, which rise into the air all around me. When they are airborne, I see most of them are quite young, still spotted and with feathered necks. One can't yet fly and instead uses my path, bounding from left to right leg in front of me as I unwittingly drive it further into the woods. I have done the same dance with a deer.

Sister has her face deep in the earth. All the way to her eyes it is buried and clumps of dirt stick between the hairs of her snout. With her sharp bottom teeth she nibbles a white tuber. This root is crunchy, white as snow, and tastes faintly of cucumber. While chewing she breathes out forcibly into the dirt cocoon she has dug. Urgently, she deciphers with her nose the long cylindrical pull of another root. Burdock. It is starchy and difficult to chew as a stick. It tastes of mineral earth and butter.

September comes even though the days of summer pass with a steadfast momentum that feels unending. We prepare a home-made dinner for Brother and Sister, their last meal. I make sweet white flour cakes with caraway seeds and dried cherries, taken from Sarah's baking cupboard. When cooked, each cake is removed from its glass baking dish and put onto a square of newspaper, then given a thick frosting of peanut butter. I jam a pig-shaped cookie cutter through the flesh of a beet, summer squash, a cucumber, a collard leaf, a block of cheese, a tomato. I press the assortment of vegetal pig silhouettes into the creamy brown faces of the cakes. A friend brings a forty-ounce bottle of beer from E-Z Mart in town to go with the cake.

Sarah and I walk the food down the road, newsprint flapping ceremoniously, and through the hayfield and brambles to the pig pen to serve them. They eat in a more measured, urbane manner than normal on account of the peanut butter sticking to their thickly ridged mouths. As usual, one discovers the goodness of the beer before the other and Sister sucks most all of the malt liquor down as fast as she can in slurps that would be applauded in any beer hall. After her bowl is drained she stands stupidly, looking out at the surrounding mosaic of leaves. The pigs are handsome and we size them up, admiring, with some solemnity, Sister's spots and Brother's fat.

At noon the next day we shoot them. Ethan rolls plantain leaves and puts one in each ear. Brother is shot over his grain bowl when I'm not looking. His sister's left ear folds over protectively against the gun blast that has now dissipated and retreats into the brush, but she is lured out to continue eating. Ethan gracefully aligns the barrel above her eyes and against her thick skull and shoots. Sarah sinks a knife into Brother's throat and blood comes out in a crimson curtain. The blood has a beautiful brightness in it, making it almost orange, not like any color you normally see, but one that is secret and vivifies from unexpected exposure to light. Both pigs lie kicking for a while after they are stuck.

"They had a lot of life in them," someone says.

Brother is dragged out of the woods. Sister lies alone in dappled sunlight, her eyes closed. Projected around her is the green canopy, lit from above, a gilded ornament to her death. She was my favorite. She died with an instinctual knack for this, as for other parts of life. Her body remains warm and agreeable. I see her teeth for the first time—two surprisingly square ones in the front angled toward each other. The rest are spotty molars.

We roll up the fence and carry out the feed bowls. Both pigs are loaded, lying down, in the bucket of the tractor, and Ethan drives them back across the hayfield to the house. He raises the bucket halfway to make sure their bodies don't fall out. Sarah and I follow behind in the truck.

In the grass of the lawn, carabiners are shoved behind the tendons in their back legs and clipped into triangular gambrels chained onto the edge of the tractor's bucket. Ethan raises the bucket with the tractor's hydraulics and the pigs float up, at full two-hundred-pound extension, from their hind legs. We hose off their hides until Brother becomes more red and Sister more blond.

With knives, one pair, Ben the Sufi cook shows up to help, works on each pig simultaneously. Their skin is split across their back legs and down the centers of their stomachs until the point where their front feet begin and the width of them is again crossed with the knife. The exposed fat is white and clean. I am proud of their quality, the purity of the sugar-white fat and the delicate pink flesh neatly whole underneath. We begin the careful process of separating skin, peeling it back in an increasingly heavy sheet. The skin is held taut with one hand, while with the other, the knife scores repeatedly the seam between skin and fat, pushing it back with every stroke.

After the soft fat of the jugular is easily cut with a switchblade, the singular skin hangs twitching around the neck. Sarah then presses a bone saw into the spinal cord. Both heads are removed.

Graham has come for the pig processing, but he didn't want to see the pigs—whom he'd fed and watered on his visits—die. He didn't know how we could be so heartless, but he is there on the lawn when we return from the woods with their bodies. I bartered their death for my own freedom from husbandry, along with extra money for winter, which I quickly sink into books and time spent writing.

Graham wants to make headcheese, so we give him the head

with the cleanest shot sunk inside. The other is buried. First, he'll remove the cheek meat; then the skull is cut into a V until the baseball-sized brain is located and gently dragged out of its cavity. He finds the slug and cuts away the burnt edges where it struck. The eyes, tethered by ocular muscles, are also coaxed out of their houses. When the head has changed from blood red to fleshy pink, it is given salt and pepper in equal amounts and lowered into a pot of boiling water on a hot plate, where it will cook on the front porch all day. The house paint bubbles underneath the meat, which has turned to vapor, floating up to the heavens.

Sarah, Ethan, Ben, and I continue to work on the carcasses. A hole is cut around the anus and the bung tied off with bailing twine. Then we cut the body open. The tip of the knife works carefully between fingers in an upside-down V beneath a layer of flesh so as not to plunge into the organs, still turbulent with digestive fluids. Eventually, the cavity is entirely split, releasing the tension holding the body together.

Inside, beneath fat and skin, it is all sheen and the churning of a superior machine. The large intestine begins to lower out first, but all the organs are sewn together by a universal membrane. Exposed are the matte pink of lungs and the hidden heart. The white webbed stomach. A full bladder. The neat frills of the liver are clotted in beautiful pink- and red-patterned cells; we all stop to look and save it for the dog. The kidneys, twins of a deeper red, sit in full sun on the plywood table on our lawn and start to change. The skin encasing them becomes egg white and iridescent. We collect all the inedible pieces—the curling penis and bitter gallbladder—in two buckets and bury them in a hole.

The pig bodies, now reduced to meat, bone, and four hooves, are slipped inside contractor bags and lowered from the tractor into the truck bed. We drive them to the vegetable farm's walk-in cooler, where they will hang to cool overnight. At the farm, I pick herbs to put in the sausage we will make. My fingers, soft with fat, smell faintly of iron and the crisp oil of lovage and bitter parsley, the diesel of thyme and oregano, so sensual that I unabashedly pass the softened and perfumed palms of my hands over my nose and cheeks, sniffing politely as one who does not deserve that which I am given and that which I have taken away.

Go, Pigs, Go

Fall 2017, New Lebanon, NY

Girls in cowboy boots show black-headed sheep in the sawdust ring outside the Harvest Hall at the county fair. They all have a trained way of wedging their right foot behind the sheep's front hoof, angling the animal's frame out to the judge, deep in his review of silent criteria.

In the 4-H Hall kids have toothpicked together cars and airplanes from carved-out zucchinis, with cherry tomatoes as pilots, and displayed them on tables covered in dirt. There are winning pies, some moldering now, posters detailing rabbit husbandry, and prizewinning sunflowers displayed in an X to fit inside the one-story building.

Sue Wee Flying Pig Races are held throughout the day. Fairgoers ascend the bleachers to watch the show, holding up bread pockets filled with pepperoni and marinara sauce like chalices. "Cotton-Eye Joe" blares around the AstroTurf ring while the crimson-faced announcer warms up the crowd, standing in full sun on the balding grass. He holds a Monster can that is undoubtedly full of alcohol. The track is anchored to a trailer, and the pigs circle it as soon as a metal gate is lifted, releasing them from inside the mobile home. They are racing toward a tray covered in Oreo cookies at the end of the loop. They are tiny, pig-wise, probably only a month or two old, weighing in at thirty pounds. Some pigs run, but others mill about the track and poop while the kids watching laugh happily. "Tug o'War," the announcer says, naming a potential winner. "Nope, it's Pulled Pork!"

"That's all we got!" the announcer says loudly into his headset, then more quietly, he seems to add for himself, "Like the Energizer Bunny."

I stay fifteen minutes, until the next race starts. I like when the animals we eat are trotted out in front of us and celebrated.

"I think this crowd is good," the announcer says, face reddening.

"I think my pigs decided to take a nap," he says to the new crowd of kids. "Can we wake them up?"

"Go, pigs, go!" he hollers, getting the kids to join in with high-pitched fervor. "Go, pigs, go!" they scream. Some spectators seem to have acquired rubber pig noses, shouting with nasal abandon into the plastic snouts, "Go, pigs, go!"

"The swiftest swine this side of Seattle, they're fully trained, folks," the announcer says, pumping his arms in the air. Sweat beads around his gelled hairline.

"Snoop Hoggy Hog, Piggy Smalls, The Notorious P.I.G." In quick succession, the pigs circle the ring, still good runners at the age before their bodies grow long and heavy, and the track is emptied for the second act.

"Folks, these are Sri Lankan mountain pigs I bought from a man in a van down by the river. Not one, but two death-defying jumps," the announcer says, interrupting himself, his saliva thick in his mouth. Accordion music begins to play and a dazed cluster of spotted goats emerges from the trailer door onto the AstroTurf.

The announcer insists on calling the goats mountain pigs, telling the crowd, "These guys are fifteen weeks old, trained in two weeks." They gallop and jump with a frivolity unattainable to swine, making easy work of the miniature course.

The announcer goes out on the road with the animals from April to October. He keeps the pigs four to five months before he gets new racers, he tells me after the show. He lives with the mountain pigs and the real pigs in a "divided" trailer. "I still can smell the poop," he says. "It's something that never gets away from you." Then, sipping from his Monster drink, adds, "I managed a Yankee Candle for five years."

The fair is, as usual, excitingly amateur: children in the show ring. A woman combing the hair from an angora in her lap to spin into wool. A man tying flies under a magnifying glass. Cows trained to milk twice a day, and a herd of running pigs.

While the sun lowers, Graham and I sit in the beer tent facing out to watch the flow of men in tall-heeled work boots walk by. The teenage boys watch each other ride the mechanical bull under floodlights, their bodies rocking in muscular spasms on the block covered in cowhide.

Driving home from the fair, we see the bifurcated corn leaves turn yellow and silver in the headlights. The farm's vegetables won four blue ribbons this year: poblano peppers, white garlic, eggplant, and a cornucopia basket. Three of each variety must be submitted; they are judged on uniformity, no waxes or polishes allowed! When we get home, I half expect Brother and Sister to be in the front lawn angry over their missing dinner or wanting to discuss the weather and call me out from the house where they know I live, but only the big Maine coon Goose's eyes flash from the depths of the big forsythia bush.

The next morning on the porch, under cover from the rain, we will break down the pigs into cuts. Anxious to begin, I've already set up the vacuum sealer in the kitchen, with rolls of bags and bleach, cutting boards, and metal bowls. I moved the sawhorse table to the front porch.

Goose is the only one awake with me. Looking through milk crates of cleaning supplies, I carry him around on my shoulder before placing him on the carpet and feeding him a scoop from a trash can of kibble. I am waiting for Ethan to get up so we can drive to the farm and get the pigs from the cooler. I organize the chest freezers in the basement to make room for hundreds of pounds of pork. There is our friend's beef, last year's vegetables, freezer-burnt venison, soup bones.

We carry the pigs in plastic bags from the cooler back into the truck bed. Ethan and I stretch a tarp over them and fold it underneath the weight of their bodies so it won't blow away. At home, we again hang the pigs from the tractor's bucket, gambrels still strung between their back legs, then run a hose over their bodies, washing away dried blood coagulated at the necks and in the fat of the hams. It rains lightly, warm and gray. I can no longer tell which pig is which.

Ethan begins sawing a pig in half, from the tip of the coccyx to its open neck. The bone saw follows closely a line to the left of the spine. Ethan is careful not to stray too far into the meat, shredding it between the saw's teeth, or to angle the saw back into the spine, sawing ineffectually against vertebrae. When this does happen, a drip of bluish gray spinal fluid slowly pours out from the incision. As the saw reaches the open neck, the two sides heave apart, dangling one from each trotter. Another point of tension from the animal's body lets go. A new line of bone and flesh defines the interior halves. We carry the halved pig to the porch table. A smell of chilled flesh and dank clay hangs around the meat.

First, we saw off the feet. We are all drinking, clear tequila and Budweiser. We remove the ham, carving it off the body against the pearly femoral head. The bloody bits of neck are cut off and discarded. The cartilaginous remains of rib bones are carefully etched out of the meat. What is left of the side of pig is flipped and inspected. We carve out ham steaks (later I will pound them thin for schnitzel) and fill a bowl with fat the consistency of fudge, which we will cook and strain for lard. As we work, we stack chops, ribs, and ham steaks on cutting boards. I like working with Ethan, the way he shows me how to hold a rag over the cleaver handle and hit it with a mallet to separate each pork chop, and where to carefully carve away the bacon from the tenderloin—he can see the distinct cuts before I can.

On Labor Day, the third day of processing, I wake up beside Graham and Goose, whom Sarah and I jealously try to attract to our separate bedrooms. I prepare to make sausage. We keep a meat grinder packed in Styrofoam with each piece resting in its correct slot. There is a heavy electric motor, a metal basin where we funnel chunks of meat, an auger for spinning meat toward the blade, the blades for cutting and emulsifying, plates with sharp holes we force the meat through, plastic attachments in different widths to stretch the intestines around.

My hands and thighs are sore from lifting, positioning, cutting pork. I shuffle around the kitchen in rubber boots and boil water for coffee. Today Goose will get good meat, cooked bits of sausage and fat in his tin bowl. He will survey the grounds and eat scraps with the air of an amused hunter, death-cheated again.

There are 150 pounds of unground sausage meat. Overnight, a half-inch layer of blood settled in the bottoms of the plastic bins and canning pots where we stored the refrigerated meat. Sarah and I organize the sausage making. The vacuum sealer, Sharpie markers, and scales are clean and ready.

We drop the first chunks of unseasoned meat into the machine with the plastic plunger prodding each cube toward the interior of spinning blades. The meat comes out of pinholes in white and pink threads of fat and flesh, which we catch in a metal mixing bowl beneath the spout. When the first batch is ground, we pass it through the machine a second time and then it is packaged in one-pound bags, sealed, labeled, put into bulk crates that we carry to the basement freezers. After the first plain batch, we graduate to garlic and herb. Six or seven friends hunker around the kitchen table for an entire day. First, we drink a pot of coffee, then we start to drink beer and the cheap red wine we bought for the sausage. We are mincing garlic, parsley, oregano, mixing it with measured piles of salt and pepper and splashes of red wine vinegar over twenty-pound batches of pork. We churn the meat and spices by hand and run them through the grinder.

We soften intestines in cold water. The long white ropes with hollow centers are not from our pigs but brought in from some-where in middle America where they've been industrially cleaned and packed in salt. I take one of these long tubes and stretch it over the plastic cylinder we attach to the end of the meat grinder. It is like putting on a condom or a silk stocking, except every foot of intestine is scrunched to fit until it is condensed into a thick white bulge up and down the tube. We tie the end of the intestine into a knot. "Okay," I say. Sarah flips the grinder's ON switch and the meat shoots out into the intestine. It is my job to gently guide the intestines off the tube as they fill—trying not to overfill them, which would make them tear with the pressure of forced meat. Slowly, I spiral one long sausage over a cutting board. "Okay," I say again when the intestine runs out, and Sarah turns the machine's motor off. I twist the long tube of sausage into links, going along in six-inch sections and turning it clockwise, then counterclockwise at every other link. It is pink and white and speckled in green herbs. By day's end, the pigs exist entirely in reconstituted packages in the basement freezers. The meat will be frozen then thawed. Eaten, sold, and traded. I cannot imagine what it is to be like a hawk that hunts daily, intensifying to make the kill, then coming to its senses over and over again after satiation. Once, I slaughtered some unwanted rooster for a farmer and didn't realize till hours later my face was splattered in dried blood.

After sausage making, Graham and I drive to my grandparents' house by the Saratoga horse track for dinner. My grandfather, my mom, my sister, my stepmom, and the dog are all there. We eat steak and corn sitting around a table tucked behind the couch and the TV with liquor bottles arranged on top of it. My grandfather brings out a stack of pictures, still in the developer's envelope, from 1964. My grandmother has dark wild hair grown past her shoulders and black eyes set in a bewitching olive face; her two pale, fey children stand beside her. There is a picture of my great-grandmother, forty-seven then, in a long red dress. "The kids were what, four and five then?" my grandmother asks. Their whole family young and multiplied. "Birth control works too well these days," she says to me, unsure why I haven't had accidents like her Irish twins. She tells me, though, in fair warning of the unpredictable nature of procreation, half her family were schmucks. Her own grandmother would lock herself in the kitchen, naked save for the wet dishrags she would diaper-pin over herself, and peel potatoes all day long. "And you couldn't eat her cooking. She was a terrible cook." My stepmom is sitting on the big blue couch quietly, still mourning her mom, Joan, who died last month.

By ten o'clock I am saying goodbye to my family, meat cooler empty of the Italian sausage I brought for my grandfather. I'm almost crying and I hope they can't see the grimace on my face beneath the yellowy porch light. In the car, I cry in the dark without telling Graham, while the lights from the horse track turn the sky purple. My grandfather took me there to bet on the horses. We stood watching the animals walk between the stalls and the track, all tight muscles and wet hides. One agitated horse was forced past us, its gums bleeding against the bit. I said I wanted to learn more about animals, how they see the world. My grandfather said, Having kids changes how you see everything, would you want that? Yes, I think so, I said. Now I'm leaving my family, my pigs are gone, I've got no kids of my own and barely any money. I tell myself this is why I'm crying but I'm not totally sure what it is, everything feeling impermanent. I am caught in the recurring seasons, annually everything is built up and dismantled in their ebb and flow.

Joan headed Linda's family and held them together. My grandma has done the same. Without Joan things in her family feel fractured. So often it comes down to the matriarch, I think. In their stead, I should bear children, something to continue and to love. I admire their hard work, their young frustrations, even their mistakes. In some ways I want to be just like them. As it is, I work in the cutting down, the taking away of life, but I haven't proved myself as a participant in it. Haven't tested even if I can procreate. I watch the births and deaths and I feel like a failure, shepherding life but never giving it. Farmers talk about cows or pigs, easily dismissing those that don't mother or that have still-born litters as soon-to-be meat.

As we drive home past Albany, the buildings glow, floor by floor, straight into the clouds. The Hudson River is black and heavy below the bridge, and the moon presses against the car windows, burning up the fog.

φ

After a day spent on the farm, the gravel lot encircling the Gallup Inn remains hot in the late afternoon. Inside, it is dark with the sun dimmed from tinted windows, and the absorbent carpet swallows up the remaining electric light. A bugle call rings out from the TV, marking the beginning of a horse race. I wait alone at the bar to order a beer.

"I looked at the moon last night, it looked just like an egg," a man sitting at the bar says.

"Yeah, full moon Sunday," the woman next to him replies.

"It looked just like an egg," he says.

· Turning Stone Green ·

VI

Planting in the Quarry Town

Spring 2018, Barre, VT

Homesick, I moved in spring, happy to be back in Vermont for
this season. They say a place imprints on you and you can't help
but love it.

In May, the tamarack trees here grow in spindly stories above
farm fields scratched out from the woods. Here it is more like a
shire, not a valley, but with rolling hills so deep that the eye can
see only chunks of land before what lies beyond is obscured by
mountains. In the distance, the site of another farm on a hill:
some high-up milking parlor the size of a sugar cube. It is colder
here than in New Lebanon, the stars brighter. And there is more
trash on the farm, old equipment thrown in the woods. One
broken-down tractor, in a line of many, has the *Playboy* bunny
hand-painted in black strokes on its hood. During winters, with
all the vegetables harvested and the surviving animals congre-
gated under shelter, I live off the farm, but I always come back,
year after year, when signs of spring begin to show. Back to the
tractors, the plants, the animals, soon everything lost to ten-hour
days and the oblivion of summer.

φ

Diana and Sam, the farmers in Barre, live in a white trailer, which functions as farm office, workers' canteen, communal bathroom, egg-washing station, and bedroom. There is a TV on a shelf and a couch covered in dog hair, a pantry stocked with soft white bread and ground coffee, the fridge with gallons of half-and-half and one-pound blocks of cheese. Over everything a layer of fine grit: books, magazines, and mail browned with it.

Diana runs the farm with a sardonic sense of humor. She plants the seeds, harvests, and hauls thousands of pounds of vegetables. Sam runs the machines, his grim reaper tattoo moving beneath his shirt as he starts tractors up or takes them apart. Diana has a long black ponytail and Sam short dark hair. A white dog and a black dog live here too. They got Wendy, the white dog, for guarding the chickens, but she showed a penchant for eating their feet. Her teeth aren't actually sharp, but they're ground gray from chewing at the chain she was tethered to before being taken in here. She stowed pork fat, thrown to her by the farmers, inside her doghouse and was sleeping on top of a mountain of lard, something a dog who had been starved would do. Wendy was eventually retired and moved into the trailer, mentally unfit. Franz, the big black mutt, is simply old and also retired. He sleeps through the hot days sprawled beneath the kitchen table, waiting to lick dirty pans from the overcrowded kitchen, amongst many offerings Diana gives him.

I can see the pigs from the front door of my cabin at the edge of the woods. It is a simple room with two windows and a loft bed covered by a tin roof—it's free and my own for the season, along with a dollar-an-hour raise. From the top window, I see the open field so that my bed floats above the crops and animals in a season thick with dreams. Of course, like the trailer, everything inside is covered in dirt. The pigs live ankle-deep in shit and it smells sweet—fecal from the front steps of the cabin. One of the three hundred chickens from a big coop that looks like a covered wagon escapes into their pen. They have her huddled in a muddy corner. I think with regret they might eat her, but at the last moment she jumps from the muck and runs, her head tilting like a javelin, diagonally out of the corner and right through a square in the woven-wire fence.

The chickens, as a group, make a slow and curdling chorus parallel to the pigs, who bark at one another. My cabin triangulates their pens. Like an ornament atop this configuration, the bright planet of Jupiter shines just above the farmers' white trailer, making it seem like a cloud. At dusk bats dart over the chickens, who roam their fenced-in pasture for grubs. In the day, crows pester them, flying in threes.

There is a shooting range on the adjacent property and the days are filled with blasts, incredible sounds so that we can't tell if they are using dynamite in the nearby granite quarry or shooting into hay bales. There is a waiting list to be a member of the gun club. Between the shots, I can hear the pigs breathing, the metronomic buzz of the electric fence, and the timed cycle in which the walk-in cooler in the big unpainted barn turns off and on.

It is still mud season in Vermont, winter's brown thaw, and there isn't much fresh food yet. I pick dandelion greens and boil eggs on the stove in the farmers' trailer while the poultry manager, Chris, runs the egg washer, hooked onto the kitchen sink. Chris is well over six feet and smiles easily, revealing a missing front tooth. All summer he works alone in a dirty Waffle House hat and sleeveless shirt. He lives in downtown Barre, sometimes with a girlfriend, but always with his female pit bull, Bandit. Chris places the shit-covered eggs from the three hundred chickens on a small conveyor belt, which transports them into a silver box. They are sprayed down inside so that they roll out from the other end beige and clean. Chris stacks them wet in plastic flats, working both hands simultaneously over the shining eggs, sometimes diverting a hand toward a bucket on the floor to throw a cracked egg.

The farm is on the town line between Barre and Plainfield, tucked into the foothills. The WPA guide written in the 1930s can still, for the most part, accurately describe the area. "From the air," the guide says, "Barre appears as a cluster of dwellings and long sheds by the railroad, with the shattered mass of Millstone Hill, great slices of which have been devoured by fifty years of quarrying . . .

"Main Street Barre is paved with granite blocks and lined on either side with close-set places of business, dingy buildings masked by colored fronts, gilt signs, and show windows. To enter this long narrow stretch from the open countryside is to come suddenly upon a virile little city transplanted from some busier section into the heart of rural Vermont."

There's Beverage Baron, the liquor store; and Mulligan's, the bar with half-price burger night; the local library; and the Snack Shack, which serves big pink cones of strawberry hard pack. Everyone who makes their home in the now depressed town itself (once rich off the granite quarries), instead of on the network of dirt roads and farms, lives in peeling Victorian houses or Victorian houses cut into apartments. One has a Confederate flag in front of it. On Main Street, there are empty storefronts and a vape shop, bagel store, sub shop, movie theater, and Bada Bing, one of the state's only strip clubs. Diana pointed out the cemetery full of granite headstones. She said to watch out 'cause the cops hide behind the big granite gates; then she pointed across the street to the flat spot where the town dumps its snow in winter.

The town library is on the way to the home of Steve and Genevieve, my good friends who moved from Northern Vermont, where we once all lived—and so is the bookstore, where Genevieve works, across the road from a steep drop-off to the river. That summer, I buy many books from Genevieve, often dressed in cotton frocks, silver glasses shining from between brown flowing locks. Though they're old friends, I never invite her or Steve to the farm because they are governed by principles of beauty and I'm worried they'll find the trailer with its coating of dirt and dog hair ugly and chaotic, but really they wouldn't mind. Before I came to their house in Plainfield, Genevieve described it to me in letters,

> *let me fill you in on my surroundings. in my barn studio, surrounded by paintings, pigments, magical talismans, papers, books; the heavy rough-hewn barn door is cast open on its rusty hinges & the world (grasses, flowers, singing birds, buzzing flies, rushing stream, hissing, sizzling heat!) is right there . . . comes in through even . . . the sun comes right in as does the wind & the flies.*

Inside the house Steve's piano is stuck beside red velvet reading chairs. Crowded bookcases cohabitate with many objects, including electronics draped dramatically by cloth (a hat hides the gas meter outside), a crystal ball, a death mask, Hogarth's *Analysis of Beauty,* and a printing press. Though it sounds grandiose, the house is not stuffy, but rather enthusiastically stuffed.

"Beautiful things deserve a more dominant place and proportion in one's surroundings, practical and utilitarian things a more recessive role," states their manifesto.

I come for dinner on a hot day. Beyond the front door Steve is sitting in a black armchair shirtless, enjoying a carrot, his white ring of hair, and matching mustache, fluffy with heat.

Pleasurability is the supreme ability.

Genevieve is busy in the kitchen frying fish in butter and herbs from her garden and preparing salad with fresh peas. Her brown hair, unmarked by gray, youthful in the way of scholars and idealists, is wound into long coils and pinned to the top of her head. Clattering wooden spoons ring from the metal stovetop, I hear humming, and the flash of her skirts travels from the open passageway to the dining room.

Steve lights a match and touches it to two candles on the unsteady dinner table. We talk, not too much about the farm besides a quick report of what's growing. Steve is working on a collection of aphorisms, Genevieve on one of essays and also translations. Though they both have to work outside of their painting and reading and writing and piano practicing, they believe in doing it as minimally as possible—something I find both admirable and foreign—a wintertime ambition at least.

"I've been caught up in my Musil theater translation," Genevieve tells me, chewing her fish at the dinner table. "It grew gigantically beneath my helpless screen-weary eyes, as I discovered more and more material.

"I need to learn more about twentieth-century theater to write an introduction to the book, and there are piles of things to read for that purpose. Really, though, my heart is longing to study German Romantic ideas about wholeness in Nature and also to return to ancient Greek," she says.

Steve tells me enthusiastically, "You must listen to *The Curse of the Golden Turnip* on the radio!" and has me into the parlor to hear a new favorite CD and drink jasmine tea with the dark curtains drawn in their artists' hermitage, where he keeps a small dish of Goldfish crackers eternally stocked. I leave with an armload of books on borrow from the house and some of Genevieve's rhubarb.

After describing her study Genevieve wrote to me,

> *There is so much in there to talk about, I should make a list . . . No, the computer is not like a flower. Because it does not Become. Or does it? Endlessly regenerating, proliferating? We'll have to think about this. Are the seemingly infinite combinations self-generated by a computer mind DIFFERENT from those self-generated by Nature, which or who seems to give birth to different seeds, choosing or neglecting, that are always there, waiting in infinity, to be born? . . . But somehow, somewhere, it all connects back to the universal—as in Goethe's Urpflanze—Alles ist Blatt—everything is leaf*

I ask her if it's boring to write about season after season, if that could really be the plot of a book.

"Nature's drama is cyclical," she writes to me, "but does not get boring because of it, does it? Well, maybe we need the personal-finite-mortal to take an interest in the eternal repeating cycle that will one day go on without us & that went on without us beforehand?"

There are two other farmhands who work with me here, Lee and Bet. Lee had years of punk wandering before coming here and marrying Chris, which didn't last. Lee's covered in homemade tattoos, drives the tractors on the farm in wraparound shades to protect their blue eyes and dotes on their Belgian shepherd, dousing her in perfume, then telling the dog she smells like an expensive whore. Lee lives on the property in a cabin too. Bet lives a few towns over with the flock of sheep she cares for in the wee hours before work. She shows up to the farm in her red truck with a turkey talon hanging off the rearview mirror, an XL Red Bull in the cup holder or a box of Dunkin' Donuts for us on the front seat. She is the youngest of us all.

In the mornings we harvest wild fiddleheads to sell at market, a way to supplement the no-money spring on the farm. In April the snow melted, then the rain came, flooding the river so that farm fields were covered in chunks of ice carried out on the tide. By May, the wild plants fare better in the uncertain frost and thaw of spring. The farm is designed to run on a shoestring, and to make extra cash, everything is packed and trucked down to New York City, where the customers have deeper pockets and don't all have a vegetable garden, a rototiller, and a few chickens at home. And the chefs think a carrot from Vermont somehow has a better origin. "It's sweeter," they claim, because we get harder frosts, and the fiddleheads are firmer, more nutrient-dense, as if the cold weather itself were a kind of super fertilizer or crown.

The crew goes out in the farm truck and hikes into spots on the banks of the Winooski River that Diana has memorized. We carry white grain sacks to fill. A full one could be fifteen to sixteen pounds, sold for over ten dollars a pound. We walk across a train track bridge, behind an abandoned house, an Agway, and a backhoe toward the silty river.

In spring, being on the riverbank is like walking out to sea at low tide, sandy and sparse. By summer, this area will be thick with ferns up to our arms and the thorns of multiflora roses. Ferns grow primordially; fully formed they simply unroll upward, breaking to pieces a slippery brown husk that protects the bud.

Before the frond unfurls it is a green disk, a spiral of stem, larger than a silver dollar. This is what we pick. The early verdant green of spring piles up in these disks as we fill our sacks into bright concentrations.

These fronds grow from muddy clumps, the dead stalks of last summer's ferns. Pressed against the mud around the new growth, leached fronds and brown rattling spores from a fertile offshoot of the plant appear, spores older in design than animal sex. The fiddleheads are not alone on the riverbanks. The skunk cabbages outpace them every year. Beginning as shoots in snow, their leaves are deeply furrowed now, like those of lilies, and their smell has mellowed from rot to the sting of garlic. All around it is wet. The beavers have made terraced pools, filtered through stick dams. We know the deer have been through here to eat the ferns too because their tracks mark the wet ground. The angelica has started to flower in pretty globes of yellow-green; settlers would candy their roots to make a strange celery-tasting confection. A turtle. A duck. A goose egg. A pile of turkey feathers.

I begin to see signs of fiddleheads everywhere. I notice them from the sides of roads. But restraint. Many are still too small, fragile and quarter sized. They will get plumper, garner more per pound if we wait.

Back at the farm, there is one chicken that lives outside of its fence, mostly on the border of the pig pen, preferring the edge of sod that the pigs cleared around their fenced perimeter and, perhaps, their strange company. I look through the woven wire—right angles collapse on themselves in the checkered pattern—just to make sure she is not inside the pig pen again, for surely they will eat her this time. They have been trained to do as much. Dead chickens are flung into their pen at irregular intervals when they succumb. Some of the birds are three years old now, old for a chicken.

The free chicken has been laying her eggs in a pile of old manure, in a crevice in the dried dung. Wendy the dog sticks her white paw in the crevice and rolls an egg inquisitively without cracking it. Food?

At every meal, we eat mustard greens. Mustard greens and last year's potatoes. Mustard greens and canned beans. Mustard greens and hot grits. It is early June now, and there is still a feeling of scarcity while we wait for the returns of summer to come in.

The only things fit to harvest are wild, but the threat of frost subsides and we begin to plant. I push the walk-behind seeder for Diana when her legs grow sore, sowing purple carrot seeds. I pour them carefully into the plastic hopper of the seeder, a series of wheels and brushes followed by a tiny shoe, which covers the seeds over with dirt as they scatter—it runs on the simple inertia of gears propelled forward. All the seeds come in paper packets. In green ink they say how many days it takes for the plants to reach maturity, when they can be harvested and sold. The carrot seeds, little tan slivers and almost smelling of flowers, will sprout the fine green hairs of carrot tops within a week. I test the device on a piece of paper to make sure the seeds are coming out, then begin to travel up and down the rows, my hands gripped around the seeder's handles.

I spend whole days in a cool garage room seeding trays of vegetables, which will start in the greenhouse before we plant them in the field, and listening to Vermont Public Radio cycle through the same weather report, national and local stories, grasping square radicchio seeds and delicately placing one per cell in a large grid. Every piece is minute, planned, laborious. Diana gives me notes at the breakfast table with exactly how many trays to seed, calculated for every foot of the farm, plus extra for die-off.

The cucumbers graduate from one greenhouse to another. At this point, most of them have four leaves, two waxy planes encompassing two jagged inner ones covered in fine white hair. Their stems grow into cool green straws. Everything is watered with fish fertilizer, a cloudy brown that, like most fertilizer, gives off an unwelcome smell, both sour and sweet. Inevitably, some seedlings dry out and die, leaving leached leaves stuck to the dirt, still trying to drink. The walls of the greenhouse are hung in fine white mesh so the beetles can't get in.

Most plants don't spend all of their lives in a greenhouse and are transplanted to the field. We sit in black seats towed behind the tractor, shoving plants into predrilled holes in the dirt as we are pulled along. Sam, Diana, and I work from eight to eight planting winter squash and trying to coax the irrigation pump to carry water up from the river and into the fields. After we are done, row after row of leggy squash plants fans out across the field.

We transplant tiny lettuces in neat lines from behind the tractor, alongside radicchio, fennel, and spring cabbage. Slowly the farm is covered with plants moving from greenhouse to field, seed to sprout. Other greenhouses are filled with new tomato plants and the fields with greens, whose widening circumferences turn the landscape green, while the heavier vegetables of fall begin to set root.

It takes us all day to plant seed potatoes, which are last year's crop, thousands of them—pink, red, yellow, and blue—quartered and covered in budding "eyes." What look like no more than scabs will grow into whole new plants. Everyone plants—Lee, Diana, Bet, and I. The old tubers pass through our hands and are pressed into the tilled earth over and over, row after row. These will become the rotting roots of the new plants, the hosts. First will come their leaves, green and smelling of nightshade, like a stinkbug, a bittering of the soil above ground. Amongst the green leaves they'll flower in small white blooms, but below they turn soil to cream as the thin tubers fatten into fleshy potatoes. When we dig up the plants in the fall, they will be heavy with underground potatoes, round and multiplied in the dirt that they displaced to form starchy globes. When washed they glow. For today, they go dormant into the earth. They will grow in a rented field near the chickens and alongside the Winooski River, hidden by trees and poison ivy. We rake them over, bed after bed. A thin covering of soil before they will be hilled by the tractor and buried, as they like, into rich mounds of earth.

After work we get gas station cheeseburgers and fries at Maplefields, two dollars after 5:00 p.m. I unfold the tinfoil, dress my burger in a thick layer of all the sauce packets offered, and eat it in the back seat of the truck, sharing a bottle of wine with Diana and Lee. Hot from the collected heat of the day, we go swimming at Coburn Pond, the local swim spot. Through the surrounding grass, the old cement truck scales are still visible from when this, too, was a quarry. A shirtless man helps his kids fish. A beaver's slick head crests the water like a greasy cork. I dive and come up to the surface, the meniscus of the world ever present. Punks from the trailer park are sitting on the bank and Diana offers them free potatoes from last season, since now we have the promise of more.

A few days later, crows dig them up, unseen. They eat holes through the starchy quartered potatoes or simply grasp them in their shining beaks and joyously throw them around in the dirt so that we have to go back, reseed and re-cover everything.

Bugs work their devastation in different patterns, on a smaller scale. They move plant to plant, leaf to leaf. Leaf miners burrow into a row of chard, leaving transparent channels in the leaves and rendering them unsalable. We go through squishing them with an air of futility. I fill the pockets of my windbreaker with the infested leaves and later find them rotted into a pulp there. And there are potato beetles on the eggplant and peppers. We take the fat red-and-black-striped grubs between our fingers and squeeze until they're so tight with watery guts they burst orange, but we can't go through all the plants. There's simply too much. Instead we bet the damage can be sustained. We bet over and over again the plants will make it long enough to bear fruit or reach maturity. Slugs mob the radicchio crop, eating the outer leaves to confetti. We hope there is enough of the hearts left to sell. Green hornworms will creep along the smooth surfaces of tomatoes and puncture their skin with the fang-like horns on the tops of their heads. Once the fruit is exposed, they attach their soft mouths to it and eat into the tomato, leaving trails of green excrement that look like tiny grenades. For every vegetable, there is a favored bug. The cabbage has its moth, white and dancing amongst the fields, but its caterpillar is a green scourge upon the plant, eating through layers of waxy leaves and pooping them out in frenzied trails.

VII

Luke

Early Summer 2018, Barre, VT

Luke, a co-worker of mine from nearly ten years ago (going from farm to farm, he is a lot of people's old co-worker), is hired on as a delivery driver to bring our vegetables down to the New York City market. He looks the same now when he comes into the trailer during dinner as when we first worked together. He remains short and brown-blond-haired with a mustache over his upper lip, a tongue piercing, a necklace tucked beneath a white T-shirt, and cargo shorts. We worked on a farm that grew so many carrots we'd spend most of October and November picking, topping, washing, and sorting them. After work at the bar or in our beds, we could close our eyes and still see orange shapes on the sorting table, moving down the incline.

Bad luck always seems to court Luke, or he it. He masterfully fashions complex fixes to simple problems. I saw him catch on fire using a propane torch to burn off weeds. His shredded and grease-covered work pants ignited like a wick. The burns healed but he kept having nightmares about it, the flames, being swallowed and killed in them. I took Luke to the hospital when he dropped a steel tractor attachment onto his foot, which had swelled into an egg by the time a doctor saw him. Luke's car always shit the bed, bingo hall money went missing around him; there were defaulted loans, failed loves, FarmersOnly.com dates, drinking and pills, not drinking and pills, which I don't know much about, except that he broke his heel once and maybe liked the medicine too much. Luke always had some kind of job though, unlike the people who would appear in tents at night on the farm where we worked, only to disappear in the morning. Sometimes we plowed up syringes in the dirt.

Luke once told me bluntly, "At least you were born with the right parts," meaning I was born a girl and wanted to keep being one, not like him.

Luke had a bleeding heart for animals, which complicates life for a farmer. He once made me help him rescue a groundhog as it lay in the middle of the dirt road, arms and legs raised toward the sky and shaking uncontrollably. Its family had eaten most of our cabbage and peas that year; Luke wrapped the creature in his flannel shirt and took it home, feeding it more of our vegetables while it recovered in a cardboard box. He called the vet for help, but they said, as a rule, they don't help groundhogs.

I sometimes gave Luke rides home with his dog up the steep hill and away from the Winooski River. Often they wore matching bandannas. One day when I stopped to pick him up because his car inevitably had broken down, he said he'd been crying. He was wearing sunglasses, but I would have known anyway as he said, sniffling, "The vet says Sully only has a few months to live." He said Sully had a tumor.

"Is he feeling bad?" I asked.

"His eyes are watering," Luke said as I turned to look at the dog in the back seat, and it was true, Sully's black shiny eyes streaked the fur below in dark tears.

"It's gonna be really lonely without him," Luke said. Our old boss was afraid of what would happen if the dog died, knowing that Luke and Sully were each keeping the other going.

Soon after Luke gets the delivery job on Diana and Sam's farm, I have a beer with our old boss. He tells me Luke stole seven hundred dollars from the farm account this past winter when he was supposed to be farm-sitting. First it was charges at liquor stores, but by the end of the week Luke was getting cash right out of the ATM. It's bad but we're both kind of laughing about how fucked-up everything can be.

Later that week, as Diana and I go out fiddleheading, through the greening hills just the two of us, I warn her about Luke. I hate to do it, but I'm scared something bad will happen, worse than just losing money. "I just wanted to tell you so you know," I say lamely. She listens, but decides to keep him on anyway. Luke is a friend and there aren't many innocent people to do work out here that pays this little.

Then, it is just another day fiddleheading, but this time they are perfect. It is like going snow-blind, a maze of green-white curls (every living color now a hyphenated green), nearly all the unfurled fronds at an ideal eatable stage. Diana and I harvest sixty pounds into grain sacks in a few hours before she spots the game warden sitting in his truck on a road behind the railroad tracks on this unclaimed land. We leave before he sees what's in our bags. Struck with a terrible thirst, because we've gotten so hot clamoring blind through thickets on the Winooski River, Diana buys us each a Sprite at the Jiffy Mart on the drive back to the farm. It is a treat to go out like this. Comparatively, the culti-vated farm fields are harsh and ordered, no shade or cool water. And on the farm there isn't a maze of an ecosystem but just a simple human plan: here will grow a row of carrots, there one of lettuce.

A chicken is dead in the shade beneath the coop, of what I don't know. The soft down around her vent shows no blood. I crawl beneath the house on the hardened ground amongst the living birds to drag her stiff body out by a foot. I carry her hanging this way to the pig pen and drop her in, her wings catching air before her dead weight thumps down in the mud. She's pig food now. Finally, the phantom of some chicken in the pen is real.

Three of the pigs are dressed appropriately in black, the fourth is spotted. One of them gets ahold of the chicken, parading it nervously through the pen, away from its littermates. The chicken is dropped and dragged through the wallow until its entire body turns from sienna plumage to a hard impenetrable mud brown. Finally, a black pig bites at her head. A crack. Either the beak or skull is crushed and the first taste of food leaks out of her. There is the unpleasant task of plucking to be done with the mouths of these lumbering omnivores, but they parse through the feathers into breast. Now livid pink emerges from mud. The colors are changing fast. Spots stretches out the wing bone and begins to strip the flesh away. A black pig runs on stocky legs to a corner with the crumpled head and neck, separated now, to ingest all to himself. This act of wild eating makes them look even fatter than they are.

Spots has broken into the bird's cavity. The hair around her snout is yellow with the yolk of an unlaid egg. She tears open the stomach and brown processed grass and grain tumble out into the mud. Then the gizzard emerges, an iridescent clamshell. Spots begins to eat the intestines. Without good canines she can't quite cut them, instead sucking them up as a continuous thread. The cracking of bones subsides and the chicken disappears. Now it is the sucking of cartilage, nibbling and biting away what is left. This, their summer afternoon. A black pig continues to chew a foot. Their heads are all pointed down at forty-five-degree angles in abstract concentration as they saw through the tough bits.

Soon, the pigs are so big it is time to send them to the slaughterhouse. The three black pigs follow the allure of grain into the horse trailer reasonably well by 6:30 in the morning. Spots won't go. Her head smashes on the tailgate as the slaughterhouse driver and the farmers try to force her up onto the trailer. Shit rolls out of her. "Watch out," I say to the driver, and he moves his shoe before it lands. She will be loaded by force. The driver grasps one of her leathery ears and her hind foot as she screams. Her head is again thrust against the steel tailgate while she resists with her huge neck. Her blond eyelashes open then close while her head is suspended there, in a peaceful moment of sheer will. The driver and the farmers are bleeding. But Spots is forced on in the end by incremental thrusts. Once the trailer door is bolted shut Diana brings the driver a cup of coffee so that he can take a break before he pulls out of the barnyard.

After the pigs are gone, I leave my remaining companion, the wayward chicken, a crumbled cracker in the dirt, but she doesn't eat it for days. I think animals like salty processed food just like us and I scatter it near the spot where I saw her daily eggs deposited. This morning on my way into the trailer from my cabin I notice the crumbs are finally gone. In their place a bulbous white and black poop. The meal has been taken and the hen stands in the 7:00 a.m. sun near her three hundred amber-colored sisters, a nice time of day for plumage. They all came together in the mail— the post office phoning to say they'd arrived—inside cardboard boxes, peeping through airholes, fed solely on the remaining yolk that surrounded them. When hatched, they travel without further hunger or thirst for the first two days of life.

The hen sees me and begins circling my feet in the tall grass before I disappear into the trailer for a breakfast of coffee and a fried egg, one of the many cracked eggs we can't sell. At dusk after a day of hot work in the field, in the shop, in the greenhouses, I walk out the back door of the trailer with a bowl of early summer nettle soup, and again the hen surfaces from the unmowed perimeter of the fields.

Ever since the pigs were taken away to the slaughterhouse, the chicken stands at the edge of their fence looking into their pen and squawks for them. She hides in the tall grass, bleating into the empty paddock. It is mysterious to me still what they think of one another, being creatures of entirely different constitutions.

And now the chickens have gone too. The free chicken, my familiar, left an egg cracked open on the path to my cabin before being packed up in her coop and moved to a rented field a few miles away, trading in her singularity for membership in the flock. Now that the farm's animals are gone, I listen for the shy hermit thrush, never seen, sounding from the woods in a continuously alternating tune. It is both mechanical and spontaneous sounding. A chirp and thrum at home with the routine sounds of chain saws and tractors, humming motors and human activities, nearly all of it produced in little pockets of land where no one can see.

I get to know the animals more quickly than I do the other farmers, though we come to like each other. Our fondness is partially born from the dumb proximity of sharing our coffee in the morning and our beer at night and by sharing the purpose of the farm, our hard work in the same service. Plus, they have a good sense of humor. I like living with them, the people and the dogs, on top of everything growing.

The day we move the chickens, the whole crew goes to the Wayside for dinner. It is a one-hundred-year-old diner with the best homemade rolls I've ever had and maple cream pie. The menu is full of strange novelties like carrot ice cream, honeycomb beef tripe, and of course, this time of year, fiddleheads in the eggs and the shepherd's pie. "Yankee Cooking at Its Best!" Six of us stuff into a maroon booth and order pink frosted glasses of Love Potion No. 9 and chocolate milkshakes. Soon the table is filled with chicken and biscuits, platters of fried fish and clam rolls. It is fun getting big plates of cheap food and everyone's happy. When we finish, greasy and tired, Lee, the tattooed tractor driver, piles the leftovers into a box, pouring milkshakes over fish strips, french fries, and bitten-up bread crust, and feeds it all to Tess, the dog, in the parking lot. We laugh as Tess eats the ugly compost of our combined dinners and watch to see which she has first. When Tess eats a Big Mac she takes the patty out of the bun, then licks the condiments, and finally eats the roll. A nimble-snouted Belgian shepherd, she's always been refined in spite of remaining an unfixed bitch.

VIII

Red, White, & Blue

Summer 2018, Barre, VT

On the summer solstice, I work pruning tomatoes. A lot of days I work alone. Lee has become sick with Lyme disease and is forced to spend sunny mornings sleeping in their hot cabin. Without Lee running the tractors, the weeds grow in fast and thick. Chris looks after his flock. Sam, Diana, and he trade market shifts, disappearing to deliver produce to New York City twice a week. Bet spends her days in the wash room packing vegetables or out herding sheep. Diana gives me a list of what to weed, pick, hoe, or seed at the kitchen table while we drink our Folgers.

In the greenhouse, snails are coupling, suspended by threads of mucus from the scaffolding. Wound together, their dull black eyes prick out from their amorphously twined bodies, which turn bluish in their exertions. The tomatoes grow in vining bushes toward the sunlit ceiling and with the plants' abundance comes disease. They lap it up from the bottom leaves and it climbs in yellow ringed splotches toward the tops of the plants like blots of ink.

I cut away at the tomatoes and haul the unwanted branches to a pile in the woods, away from this incubator of fruit, training up the remaining branches onto white strings hung from the ceiling so that when I am finished there are neat aisles of green leaves, the branches suspended in evenly spaced V's. At night, covered in a layer of the tomatoes' noxious sap, I sit in a lawn chair tucked into the woods by my cabin, and the temperature drops to forty-one. Most of the time there is the edge of cold here. It's not yet high summer.

But by the first of July it reaches ninety degrees in the dark of night. All week the humidity simply mounts. We start work at six in the morning and finish by three in the afternoon, too hot to continue. Instead, I lie on the floor of my cabin with pond-soaked hair. Like the plants, the weeds thrive in this weather, and the work is in pulling them out of the dirt in between days of planting and harvest. In the evening, too warm to run the trailer's oven, I drive to the Maplefields and buy an Italian sub, a can of beer, and an iced tea. I drive along the dirt roads, jade corn up to the hubcaps, and take the brown paper sack inside, where I eat on the floor with the door flung open to let the cooling evening air in. In this heat, the deli meat takes on a new suppleness and I eat the spilt pieces of salami and spicy capicola dangled from my fingers, slick with grease. Slumped against the wall, I drink the iced tea and beer in rounds. When I am finished, I crawl into bed, but the air is still thick and heavy like a tank of whey. In anticipation of the Fourth of July, fireworks pop somewhere in the humid black sky. Mice sound like rain in the walls. The lights are out in the trailer in the distance so outside there are only fireflies and the leaves of trees darker than the blue-black sky.

Luke is asleep in the barn so he can wake up in the night and start the drive to New York City. He'll be there by sunrise to set up for the market. I gave him some of my Labatt Blue from the fridge and later he texts me to see if I want to hang out with him in the hayloft but, as usual, I sleep through it, partially relieved not to see him, afraid of his mounting problems. He arrived at the farm in a small car with a bicycle rack hung over the back end as a protective measure so no one can see his license plate number. Always, he has his car set up this way, as if it could outsmart the cops. He tells me as much, but I don't ask why. It is impossible to live, to make money without a license here. I drove an entire summer to and from work on a suspended license. What else was there to do? A knowing hand at failing automobiles, Luke once took me to a junkyard to steal an inspection sticker for my car, which couldn't pass. We looked through all the Fords but could find an up-to-date sticker only on a Chevy Impala. Luke scraped it off with a razor and then stuck it right to his stomach beneath his white T-shirt so no one could see.

In the morning my nostrils are caked with dirt boogers, the kind that come from dry tilled earth, which my body tries not to ingest. There is mail for me on the breakfast table, a letter from Graham, far away and working too.

Looking up at the disco ball in the breakroom that hangs for an unknown reason, I can recognize tiny fragments of my face reflected in a few mirrored squares. I move my head in order to situate an eye directly in the middle of a single square and oddly it becomes the only square featuring any of my face. I don't know if this is some law of physics. The disco ball is not a perfect sphere anyway, I imagine. Last night I looked up at the moon and had the cheesy thought that you were looking at it too, and our locations formed a triangle.

With the no-rain heat everything has become dry. The river sinks low into its banks, the well water recedes deeper into the earth, the leaves of plants contract, and wind carries away our fields in dust-filled gusts. Diana and I pull buckwheat, an accidental seeding, from the potato field. First our speed mounts in the cooler morning, then ebbs with fatigue. Our backs humped, we dislodge the white-flowered crop by its blushing root from around the spindly potato plants, sprouted now into coarse green leaves.

On our lunch break, we go swimming in the irrigation pond dug out of a corner of the farm. We are laughing and naked. Kids of visiting friends sit slippery-wet on rocks like summer selkies at the pond's edge and watch us paddle through the warm water. For lunch we all eat at a picnic table outside the trailer since the inside has become stiflingly humid. Beneath a shade umbrella we have roast beef sandwiches on hamburger buns and store-bought potato salad instead of home-cooked food because of the low well. We save whatever water we have left to wash vegetables for the market. In the afternoon we bring out gallon jugs of water to the field to continue pulling weeds. Wendy circles the cultivated tract, friendly and in heat, before retiring to the shade, a knowing animal in summer sun.

After the workday is through, I drive an hour north along the Winooski River to see my family. Even the highways smell of the locust trees in bloom. The river flows right by the microchip factory, where I worked one winter, past the dairy farm serviced by a robotic milking machine, and out of the town limits before spilling into Lake Champlain.

On my mom's porch, my younger cousin tells me about her housecleaning job this summer. The priests are by far the worst, she says. They all live together in one house. "But the upstairs must be off-limits to the public," she says. They have the biggest liquor cabinet she's ever seen in a private home. Their rooms are piled deep with trash except the paths carved to get in and out of bed. They are all so unbelievably filthy before appearing outdoors in their white collars and black button-downs. There are many pictures of Jesus on the walls, my cousin says, but in each one he looks like an entirely different person.

On the Fourth of July, boys with buzz cuts drop from the rocks that ring the old granite quarry, release themselves into a free fall, and disappear into chalk-blue water. Their momentum continues and they sink fast. The colors of their flesh radiate against the turquoise water that fills the man-made concavity.

Cables of twisted red steel hang from the woods surrounding the quarry and sink into the water. Wooden ladders, long abandoned by quarrymen, remain lashed to rock like barnacles. This quarry appears to be rounded but really it is made up of squared pillars of rock stained white and black where large rectangles were cut away in vertical chunks. There are pine trees and a crane in the distance, plunging into a further, still-operating quarry.

Swimming past the threshold of the first quarry into the second abandoned hole, the deep water is cool. It is like swimming in hard crystal; only skimming the top of a strange kind of portal to a deeper part of the earth, one feels the newfound absence of rock. The white-brown bodies of people and the mud-colored fish look auroral swimming through the sky-blue water. The pools are the inverse of rocks where buildings and tombstones were scraped out, the negative monument. Being in this place where things are mined out, vegetables grown, cows milked, and most of it trucked away is being close to a store of fertility, fertility for life led elsewhere. In this way the countryside, flanked by empty storefronts and abandoned mills, contains riches. Rivers of milk, fields of Christmas trees, veins of granite, gallon upon gallon of sap turned to syrup. But it does not insulate from poverty. Though money is exchanged it is perhaps at a loss. Beyond the obvious cavities in the ground, so much of what is taken or sold is a depletion.

Through the woods surrounding the quarry, half-carved statues, pillars, and rocks are arranged in a kind of impromptu sculpture park. On the railroad tracks down the mountain and through town, a man with a ponytail waves red gauzy flags out the back side of a train car as it descends. The open cars contain rocks the size of dumpsters grouped together at clumsy angles. They are gray and wild, unshaped and dotted with spray-painted codes signifying their intended use. The train begins a slow wind by the Winooski River until it stops and is unloaded at the granite sheds.

In the town cemetery all the stones are carved out of the same white-gray granite from the local quarries. Here, where an average family could afford an opulent grave marker from rock common as dirt, there are six thousand graves. Columns with smiley faces on the tops—round and beaming gray. A race car, a soccer ball, a mandolin, deer running free, an eighteen-wheeler, an airplane, an easy chair. There's a mechanic with a wrench carved into his back pocket and a pack of cigarettes in his front, two rosebuds for his dead children and four leaves for the living. There is a soldier with his wife chiseled into the smoke of his cigarette and a couple propped up in bed holding hands. In the dirt near their shared grave sits a small stone for the man's second wife, after this one died. There are so many large and disembodied hands they must be the hands of God. There are hands in prayer and hands clasped together, hands wrapped around stone-colored lilies. One pair of hands grasps a wet catfish between them, holding on to the wet slipperiness of life itself.

One morning, fifteen minutes into the workday, Sam cuts his right pointer finger with an angle grinder in the dirt driveway of the trailer. He was lying beneath the giant mower, tool spinning above his face, when he started to swear, words that mixed into the sound of the grinder's motor. He came out from under the mower's metal housing holding his hand to his chest and I gave him my seat in the truck about to leave for our river field. Diana ran out from the trailer with a roll of paper towels for the car ride to the hospital, but there was hardly any blood and there was no blood in the dirt beneath the mower either. Sam's finger was cut in a neat, surgical V, which exposed the white fat and bone on its inside. It didn't bleed because the heat of the grinder cauterized as it cut. By the afternoon Sam is back driving the tractor with his finger pointing up against the steering wheel and covered in a cocoon of gauze. Suspicious of the townspeople's proclivities—babies here are ten times more likely to be born addicted to opiates than in other states—the hospital didn't give him any pain meds.

I go to feed and water the chickens in their new pasture a few miles down the hill from the farm. When I get there in the farm truck, a man across the field is operating an excavator in a gully, digging a culvert on a Sunday. He shuts the engine off, climbs from the seat, and walks up the hill toward me.

"Good morning."

"Morning, those your chickens?" he asks, blue eyes wandering toward the field.

"Yeah."

"I saw a red fox in there this morning. I chased it out, but he came right back and got a chicken."

On his early morning dig he noticed the fox low to the earth, a different red than the rust-colored flock. When I get down pasture to the chickens, five are out. I catch only two by lunging over their prickling tail feathers and smothering their wings closed in my hands. I can't catch the other three: a scrawny one, a fat healthy hen, and a medium-sized bird with white poop smeared across her neck, all darting through the trees away from me. Diana showed me once how the chickens crouch before you when they want to be mounted. She put the toe of her boot on one's back, just touching it. It stamped its feet from side to side, spreading its wings before sinking obediently to the earth. I don't find any dead birds. The fox must have carried them all away.

I collect the chickens' eggs from their big coop after dumping seventy-five pounds of feed into the dirt, shuffling my feet so as not to crush their crowding bodies. Each side of the coop lifts up to reveal a squalid row of nest boxes. In every box piles of brown eggs have appeared since yesterday. I grab them in gentle handfuls, many of the eggs still hot to the touch, and place them in a five-gallon bucket. Some nest boxes have chickens, broody and recalcitrant when I reach beneath them to try to take their eggs. *Maybe these will hatch,* they think, or they are simply ruled by the vague compulsion of nesting, and they lower their sharp beaks on my fingers, pecking me away from their eggs. Others know to watch for the cracked ones revealed as I empty the nest boxes, and they peck at the sites of orange yolk hungrily, this preferred to their usual grain. I leave a dozen eggs on the seat of the excavator's pickup parked nearby, a thank-you for chasing off the fox.

By seven on Monday morning, the farm has received seventy-five day-old turkeys in the mail. The hatchery in Pennsylvania times it perfectly, even shipping 10 percent extra birds to account for the die-off. They are put in a brooder under an amber glass bulb for warmth. The male poults have nodes on their foreheads where red wattles will grow, hanging decorously to one side of their beaks like the tassels on a graduation cap. They circle in the protected brooder in synthetic mother shine. They are covered in sand-colored stripes with Easter yellow down beneath.

Perhaps there are two dead or dying birds. They are purposefully trampled by the pink feet of the others. Three toes in their backs over and over, their eyes closing in pain like clamshells. Others just need sleep and are pecked only as a standard of classification: not dying. Already their wings are marked by marbled feathers, their beaks and feet made from the same coral cartilage. They see with one black eye at a time, one for each side of their gumball-sized heads. Their necks, now curved in preparation, will grow long. Their ears are pink crop circles carved out of fluff.

I watch them from a slit in the wood covering their incubator box, like a god or a hungry fox. Sometimes they leave the box, walking out into the greater brooder, and look up at my bigness, but I am unimportant to their newly birthed society.

By 5:15 p.m. that Friday at Beverage Baron, everyone is sharing in the happy freedom of this day, this time. Three lines form at the points of the diamond-shaped sales counter. Habitual purchases are made alongside neighbors. An employee helps me find the rum. "Maybe I'll just get the plain one," I say. "But *that* one's not on sale," he says, so I get the coconut-flavored bottle, a can of coconut cream, and a bag each of ice and potato chips. The cashier asks for my ID and when I give it to him, he says apologetically, "I didn't recognize you with your hair up," even though I've never been here before, grew up in a town further north. The woman on line behind me starts talking to me like I'm some distant acquaintance from one of the local families. I leave with a crisp paper bag in my arms and walk across the street to Dollar General to buy mousetraps and a graduation card for one of my cousins.

We all get drunk on cheap piña coladas we make in the trailer with the blender and drink them sprawled out on the couch. I go out into the night to look at the turkeys. The sky is pink with a fuzzy moon rising. The turkeys are moving with greater precision now on angular legs. Their feathers are lengthening and they can make a range of chirps to me and one another, while scuttling their feet on the wood-chip-covered floor. The red light shines over their fuzzy heads. One pecks at its own foot as if the appendage is foreign. I look through the crack of the box they nest in. Most are sitting down. A fly, materialized to eat the droppings, rattles its black body against the walls, back and forth, back and forth in rotten absorption.

The turkeys sleep piled together. The pile breathes, they are dreaming. Eyes closed, they flinch in their sleep. What have they seen of this world to make their dreams, with their waking hours spent in the mail and then boxed in this brooder? More and more birds fall into the sleeping cluster. Outside the unseen sky darkens. Some sleep with their necks twisted so that their heads rest upside down atop their wings and their chins point skyward, illuminated by the heat lamp.

Now only two are left standing. Their eyes close upward from the bottom lids. The fly hits the ceiling. Poop spurts from a turkey onto wood chips. Then there is only one chick standing. It walks amongst the sleeping, stopping to pull at the feathers of another. Already they have found little fleas to eat off one another. Already their feet are beginning to carry shit stuck to the uneven pads. Nearly all the black eyes have closed and it is only breath. Heaving yellow bodies.

I lift a sleeping bird and hold it in my hand; its warm heart beats fiercely through downy feathers like the controlled measure of a medicine dropper. Seeds, poults, eggs, dirt, vegetables, all pass through my hands with rapidity as the life cycle mounts into summer bloom.

IX

The Size of Everything

Summer 2018, Barre, VT

In the heart of the summer, Diana, Lee, Sam, Bet, Chris, and I are dwarfed by the farm, the sheer life force of it, pulled by the demands of plants and animals, pressed like blunt objects into the ground, buried in the work we have wrought. A dairy farmer told me cows—meaning milking cows twice a day every day—can either turn a person mean or make them nice. I believe this is true. You either like a cow's touch, are quick to recognize the good in their temperament, or you dock their tails for swatting your face like a fly, hate the smell of your own sweat, as if it were their manure. With vegetables, perhaps either you go into the earth and are softened by it, or you come out like thistle. It is labor that is either heart opening or hateful, but sometimes unavoidably both.

Diana and I trellis the tomatoes again. They have grown to well over five feet in the greenhouse with their leaves stinking like poison. We crawl on our hands and knees, faces brushed with pollen from the plants and arm hair stiff with it. The July heat

collects inside and everything is growing fast now. Yellow flowers dislodge from the plants and are replaced with green fruit.
They are currently hard as rocks, most the size of buttons, some
as big as Ping-Pong balls. We cut away giant branches and thin
the plants down to two main stems reaching in wide jade V's up
to the ceiling, newly liberated from the weight of so many leaves
and hung with the ornaments of unripe fruit. I love this cutting
away and shaping of the plants. A rare moment of control, orches-
trated beauty even—all in anticipation of the moment when the
tomatoes are ready to pick in full blush.

Outside, the apple trees grow fruit too, the size of quarters
now. And the wildflowers are out: Queen Anne's lace in whole
swaths of white flounces, black-eyed Susans, daisies, red and white
clover. Even the grasses are flowering and give off feathery seeds
when the wind blows.

Abundance is upon us. The pigs come back from the slaughterhouse in packages. We sell most of the good cuts but eat count-
less links of breakfast sausage and bratwurst, cooking them till fat
bubbles brown in the pan. There is a profusion of vegetables and
we hungrily eat all kinds of food prepared from them: squash casserole, radicchio pasta, cucumbers with ranch dressing, zucchini
salads, and soon thick-sliced and salted tomatoes. I can whole flats
of them and use the leftovers in everything, sauces and soups and
strange red salad dressings and drinks. Vegetables are boiled, but-
tered, cheesed, and fried. We are exhausted from the sheer weight
of produce, the production of it, but also sated.

Luke comes into the trailer during crew lunch to return the
box truck after a delivery run to New York. These are the only
times I see him, on his way to or from deliveries—never in the
fields or on the tractors. He announces it is his birthday and asks
me for a hug. For each of his birthdays in the past, he organized
an annual snail race (once the public access channel even covered

it) in which tiny snails, no more than glints of gravel, slithered down a plastic track. Everyone had to stand in close to see which snails were incrementally winning or losing. Kids usually picked the winning snail.

When I get up from the table to hug Luke, I lean into him and breathe the deep smell of whiskey in his sweat. He cries, looking at the calendar tacked to the trailer wall. His name is not on the delivery schedule for the rest of the month and he needs a paycheck badly. Diana gave him money to buy tools that never showed up. Luke's license never showed up either. He says he can't get work while we awkwardly sit at the kitchen table eating our lunch of zucchini salad. Diana says, "You're probably just tired." Later I find out the truck came back to the farm with a new dent in it and no explanation. Quietly, Luke is let go. It will be the last time I see him.

Without Luke to deliver our vegetables, the markets continue on, twice every week everything harvested and hauled down to the city. A potato can garner more per pound there, with so many restaurants to stock, so many more mouths to feed, but I don't see evidence of any great windfall brought from the city to this humble life up here. I have not seen the figures added up on paper—it is not my business and I get my paycheck like clockwork every two weeks—but I have seen the eighty-nine-cent bread product that stocks our pantry and the gashes in the walls where the copper wires were ripped out before the trailer was bought used. The choicest vegetable is always saved for the customer.

The next morning at 6:00, I lie on my green flannel sheets next to a spider sucking the innards of a wasp out from a hole in its head. I woke as the wasp was caught in the web. I turn away, and when I look back the spider has disappeared, the birds who've built their nest on the other side of the wall are screeching, and the wasp is still trapped, one of its legs lamely bending in and out. The spider is now upon a beetle. It is a simple, small spider, nothing like the colony of orb weavers beneath the trailer roof with bodies crossed in yellow and as big as thumbs. The spider rushes back to the wasp, flipping it deftly on its back. Spinning a few strands of restraint around its body, she carries the wasp to join the killed beetle she's stored, I think, but instead she passes the beetle and disappears with the body into a green fold of the sheet and then further into the crack of the windowsill.

We observe the weekend on the farm and everyone's away and off the clock. Graham stays over. Separated by hundreds of miles of country, I've missed him. He comes back to me taller and hairier than I'd remembered. In the rare calm we make love beneath an apple tree. Our two bodies are bleached white by the morning sun, shining like whole fish; the flies swim around us iridescent as a single scale. The ground is littered with small green apples from the tree, fallen too soon. Our eyes too are part of the light, luminous browns reflecting one another. Gun blasts sound from the firing range, hidden so there is no reason to the shots and instead they come across as a great loud bass, the heartbeat of the property. With the sun on our backs, he pulls out and his seed is spilt on our bodies and in the dirt, so that no baby will come of it. Farming is often like this too; most things are picked or culled in first bloom, seldom allowing plants to go to seed, and there is no rooster for the chickens.

After, I pick zucchini before the heat intensifies. Leave them unpicked over the weekend and they become monstrous and unsalable. The rows of spiked leaves pull on my arms, my shoulders, and calves, covering them in tiny scratches, red and puffy. I have a white tub strapped to my chest so that the green fruits can be picked expediently and placed, rotting end blossoms removed, into the tub. For the better part of an hour my head remains stuck in the two-foot canopy of leaves traveling down the rows. As I pick, my hair, hanging into the plants, becomes tangled with pollen and its attendant bees, and a carpet of thistle, everything pulling me toward earth.

Thunder Road

Summer's End 2018, Barre, VT

Inside the brooder between the farmers' trailer, a blue school bus, and woods the mail-order turkeys have grown more handsome, their bodies tapered instead of downy. Eight inches tall and their plumage is lightening. Their long inquisitive necks operate like man-made cranes and their eyes have gained a new intelligence, the hazel irises deepening around dark pupils. At a time of life before meat sits heavy on the bone, the birds have chiseled a hole in the floor of their brooder and learned to escape. They funnel through the hole into the outside and flap their small wings, climbing onto the pitched metal roof of the brooder only to slide off the slant and flutter back down to earth, from where they continue to test their newfound power of flight, rising and falling.

At the Barre racetrack, a natural amphitheater folded into the mountains—"The Nation's Site of Excitement"—drivers test their own powers, whipping cars around turns at mounting speed. People sit on the big green bowl of lawn and look down at the paved ring, which is like a chip out of the forested hills. A pair of white-haired boys play in a stand of white birch, arms stretched between the thin silvery trunks so that their small stomachs jut out in front of them. Their family sits in folding chairs and on the grass around them smoking cigarettes at dusk, the smoke rising through the trees. Everyone sitting on the hill throws their empties, letting them roll into a pile for someone to collect. I recognize someone I went to grade school with and his grandpa, but I'm too shy to say hi. I'm here with Chris, his girlfriend, Lee, Bet, and a huge supply of cheese-flavored chips and beer (limit two six-packs per person). The slant of a Vermont accent comes from the announcer out of the megaphones perched on poles around the track.

The beer cans thrown down the natural incline of the lawn collect in piles in the grass. One of ours rolls into a teenager's back where he sits with his arm stretched around a girl. He brushes it off and, turning slowly, says "Fuck you," which is legible only from the shape of his lips; the sound that travels is that of car engines.

All night, the race cars float around the ring like wagging tails, snapping back to formation around turns. Inside the cars, the heat rises to nearly 150 degrees. There are sparks and flames beneath car bodies and burnouts into the hillside. A tow truck comes for them. An ambulance comes for them. Phil Scott, Vermont's governor, is driving a car that is booed as it revolves. Booed for the new gun restrictions he passed. A son of Barre, where he's won two kiss-the-cow Milk Bowl competitions, he's raced for nearly thirty years, since his mother got him into the sport when he was a child. As governor, he wants to lower taxes, legalize weed, and get the population of the graying state up to 700,000. He almost didn't come tonight, worried his new law would garner protests and ruin the show, but there is only a curdling of distrust and he doesn't place anyway, coming in fifth.

We go home kind of drunk on dark dirt roads, the world growing quiet as I drive away from the track and back to the farm.

$\wp$

Bang! Bang! Bang! Three shotgun slugs rip through the heavy silence of night. When I see Sam coming out of the trailer bathroom the next morning and crossing back into his and Diana's cramped bedroom, I ask, "Did you kill anything?"

"No," he says, "but not as many deer came back."

The animals eat through our fields, carelessly displacing rows of carrots and lettuce. On top of this scourge, for days and weeks it doesn't rain, and when it does it's not enough to satisfy the thirst of the land—just a thin smattering of water quickly absorbed into the topsoil. The well runs dry over and over, and everything is covered in dust: the roads, the fields, the vegetables. We have to flush the toilet with water from the shallowing irrigation pond and buy big plastic jugs of water for drinking. We go to the House of Tang buffet for dinner when all the dishes are dirty in the trailer and there's no water to cook or clean with. When I pay for egg rolls and Jell-O, eaten alongside kids with rattails and teenagers with their moms, I notice there's a fish tank beside the register that holds a gray fish the size of a dumbbell, so big his sides press against the glass.

Sam drives us home from the buffet onto the farm only to discover there are shapes in the fence, lightly discernible from the darkening slate-colored sky. Dust from the rainless field rises and looks green in the headlights. Paired eyes reflect in a clump from the lettuce patch. Enough eyes for five deer. The dust rises in thicker and thicker sheets as we chase them in the truck, battering our own fence and field, before they bound into the shelter of the surrounding wood. "They'll be back," Sam says. He should sleep out with his gun, he thinks.

That night I dream about a bull moose awkward and closed

in a paddock, its long gangly legs pressed against the earth as if that too was a kind of tank or cage.

While we sleep, another break-in occurs: a juvenile great horned owl gets into the brooder. It kills one turkey, but by morning, when Chris opens the brooder door, it is cornered by the hissing flock. It looks small and feral before Chris takes it out in his balled-up sweatshirt. Young bears are out looking for food too, naïvely climbing through human encampments. On the road I see a Cooper's hawk with its breastbone pointing sharply from its chest, a sign of hunger. It stands perched on a roadkill red squirrel, the body too heavy to move. The hawk rises with red fur bunched in its talons, just lifting off the road, only to sink back down to earth, hopping with the heavy weight. It stands too close to where cars turn the corner, its senses temporarily muddled by this miracle gift of food.

Of course, the deer return, this time eating the leaves of pepper plants. At dusk Diana works in a yellow rain slicker spraying pigs' blood, the powdered kind you can buy in a box, from a backpack sprayer around the perimeter of the vegetable field until her rain suit turns the color of rust and the dry ground is stained with blood. A smell to scare the deer away.

I walk out of the trailer into the driveway and see a black form, Franz the black dog, I think, but it's a bear, slow and silent, a young male with ears comically round atop an underfed body. This is the time when they are pushed out of the den to fend for themselves, and the smell of blood misting the air all around the farm fields signals nourishment to him. He looks at me from all fours. His fur is new and velveteen, deep black. He moves his torso one way and then the other and looks down his snout at the farm: the greenhouses, the trailer, barn, and fields, machines midrepair in the dirt driveway. In no great rush he turns, like a shining ribbon, and walks past a tractor and then a boulder and into the hedgerow and the tall tamarack trees.

There is an original play put on at the old town hall, the basement now a makeshift dressing room, and the meeting room a stage. Wooden benches arranged in the hall are heavy with people, babies and kids with funny haircuts alongside grandmas in wool sweaters with long gray hair and the aged playwright propped up in a corner. The play is a musical about seafaring, something entirely unrelated to life here except that it's also a love story. The cast is of all ages and assembled from town. Teenagers, costumed in white flowing clothes and ghostly makeup, play "people fish," the dead who've drowned at sea. They beckon to the sailors, dancing across the creaking wooden floors, swishing their arms, and cooing, "We are the people fish." A pirate with two missing fingers on his left hand steers his ship through the underwater sirens. The man who plays the wind personified, blowing the sails, is missing a section of his middle finger. It is pure fantasy, but farm and work accidents are all on display tonight. The wind wears a blue silk cape tied around his neck and looped around his intact pointer fingers so that he can wave it in a kind of self-propelled weather. The stub of a finger lies against the others as he flies around the town hall singing, and the audience watches from the hard benches as his cape billows and a storm builds all around them.

Back on the farm, the gray-black sky sweeps overhead, like a broom pushed by a great gust. Loosened insulation panels blow against the greenhouses. The power goes out and the egg washer stops, mid egg. The sky looks like it has fallen off a cliff and finally, as if drawn by the townspeople's song, the rain comes.

In the dark rain-cooled night, the turkeys are passed from the brooder over a piece of plywood and counted. It's after dinner and the sun is setting, a time when the birds are calm. Chris stands below the front step of the henhouse and takes each dangling turkey from Sam. "Thirty-five," he says, nestling the bird in his large hands and cutting a fine white triangle from each wing. There is no blood, only what I imagine to be the feeling of a nail cut too close to the skin. A new and unwelcome lightness. White wingtips cover the ground. The scissors work in pairs of wings then pause as each bird is passed. *Snip-snip, snip-snip, snip-snip,* ensuring they cannot get away. Briefly, summer's protestations of the harvest are blunted in rain and blood, the sounding of shotguns and the taking of flight feathers.

We harvest for most of the day before the market. The greens are the first to be picked, before they succumb to the heat of the day. I count rubber bands out and stack them on my pinkie, releasing them one at a time to bunch basil, orach, cilantro, agretti. Next, I pick tomatoes from the greenhouses; they grow unbearably warm with the lengthening day. It takes me three hours after lunch to pick twelve boxes of zucchini, traveling up and down the rows and cutting them at the stem. I harvest them until the tub strapped to me is so full I can barely bend and have to empty it into a crate, carefully lining the delicate squash in alternating rows. With the produce harvested, washed, and packed by 7:00 p.m., Chris and I climb into the box truck parked in front of the trailer, its nose pointing down the long drive, to go to the Union Square farmers' market in New York. I buckle in as Chris releases the air brake and the truck sighs into motion. I've always stayed back to do field work, but this week I come along with my plastic suitcase and maple leaf quilt shoved in the back seat. I'm not coming back, but moving in with Graham. My last paycheck will be mailed to his apartment, as if this season were a dream. Diana says I should stay, and part of me believes her, but I go anyway, watching the white trailer recede in the side-view mirrors of the big truck.

On the way to I-89 we stop at a Maplefields with a whole plaza of truck pumps. Through the automatic doors there's a mural carved in granite of men hauling buckets of sap from sugar maples with the Rock of Ages quarry stamp on it. Chris buys two Monster Energy drinks and I get a bag of chips. Luke probably would've bought a Coke, I think. We drive south under the gray evening sky. An hour passes before a small black bear bounds across the highway, hind legs nearly overtaking its front paws in leaps. We traverse the darkening Green Mountains in grades up and down on roads blasted out from the rocks here in the 1960s.

By midnight we are in Connecticut. Chris parks the truck in front of a church and we sleep on a friend's kitchen floor for a few hours, waking up to an alarm at ten of four (Diana tells me to make sure Chris wakes up because he slept through the alarm last week). We go outside, silent and tired, into the darkness and back inside the truck. Chris opens one of the energy drinks, this one red, and takes his first sip. The roads are empty and we follow them like a continuous spool of blacktop. It is still dark when the city skyline reveals itself. Once we get into Harlem there is a kind of granular half-light. By 5:30 the outline of the odd person dots the sidewalks, which seem to flatten out and pave over everything until they meet the lips of buildings and subside. None of it looks real. "Have we hit a red light yet?" Chris asks. "No," I say, and we glide along Seventeenth Street between the lights popping green until we get to Union Square, where the market will begin after sunrise. Chris backs over the curb, smooshing down the gas pedal, forcing the back wheels to mount the cobblestone square, and he squeezes past a trash can and into the farm's designated spot at the market. With the truck in place we sleep for another ten minutes. Sleep pulls on my eyelids until Chris's alarm chirps on again.

We get out of the truck and a man with long black hair passes slowly through the square. He is not one of the bustling workers setting up their wares. He carries a dead goldfinch in his left hand, dreamlike. No one pays attention to him. He lets the dead bird lie there in his palm as if it will come back to life.

Chris and I take out the tent poles from the trailer and the cement weights that keep them from blowing over. We piece together the roof poles (their whole setup is homemade) and stretch the white shade tarp across them, put in the spindly steel legs to stand it up, bring out the sawhorses and wooden table-tops, set up the scales and cashbox. Once the U-shaped booth is arranged, we haul out boxes of cabbage; beets; tomatillos; basil; chard; frisée; carrots; zucchini; red, purple and orange tomatoes; white and blue potatoes. All stacked in alluring piles. Surrounding us, the other farmers do the same. At 8:00, we open.

It's Saturday, and the chefs and serious buyers are out first with rolling carts to fill. Chris and I stand behind the tables of vege-tables, weighing produce, filling Thank You bags, making change, and writing up receipts. By ten there's a protest. First the chants are unintelligible, but the protesters wind down the block paral-lel to our stand in front of a McDonald's. "There's no excuse!" they call out, only to reply, "For animal abuse!" The farmer with arthritic hands selling maple syrup shakes his head as does a New Jersey grower adding tomatoes to a pyramid. The customers seem unfazed. There is a protest nearly every market day here.

I take my lunch break and eat sushi in a cool dark cafeteria away from the noise and heat of the street. I return to the stand with a Coke to help curb the pull toward sleep after the work of yesterday's harvest. Chris locks himself in the truck to nap while I work so he can stay awake driving back to Vermont alone tonight.

After so many days on the farm, I am shocked by the profusion of people at the market. From Plainfield, a town of twelve hundred, to a square visited by sixty thousand. A man with legs like a stork carries a bouquet of hydrangeas balanced atop his cane. Another man dips into the stand drinking a water bottle full of red wine. There are people in all-jean outfits, dresses, platform sneakers. People shopping with assistants who carry their new houseplants, loaves of bread, and cheese wrapped in white paper. A woman with thin arms comes up to our stand, where I idle behind the scale. "Ooh, you're dirty," she says, smiling, eyes roving down my white tank top, loose and covered in brown smudges, the cracks of my hands, wrapped around the cool Coke can, alive with soil. "I like to roll around in the dirt like a pig," she tells me, batting sea-glass eyes. I bring the can to my lips and sip. "Oh nooo! You'll feel the difference once you're healthier," she tells me, looking at the soda tragically. "You need Coca-Cola and beer to work," I say, "but I eat lots of vegetables." She buys a bunch of yellow beets before disappearing back into the street. "Animals love their families!" "Just like us!" the protesters chant. But nothing stops the flow of commerce. By one o'clock our entire cooler of eggs is sold out.

The piles of vegetables grow smaller and smaller as people come in and go out of the stand. After five we begin to box up what is left. We load the unsold flats of tomatoes and boxes of potatoes onto the truck, stow away the cashbox and scale, take down the tent, and sweep the emptied stall. Everything disassembled, Chris starts the truck for the drive north. I walk across the square and go down the stairs into the subway.

XI

The Funeral

Winter 2019, New York, NY

In January, Diana called to ask if I'd heard Luke was dead. He killed himself, she said. I didn't ask how and she didn't say. Later I found out it was on an animal farm up north. He spent the morning up on a ladder fixing a roof or maybe some siding and two hours after working together his boss found him dead. I cried, but I was not wholly surprised; instead I felt the shame of knowing, yes, he might have done it. That he felt cornered and desperate, I knew. I don't know if his suicide can be counted alongside the dairy farmers who have been killing themselves, hopeless and in debt. Farmhands don't even count in these equations, they have already been disinherited from owning anything, and Luke had other problems.

I drive with Graham to Luke's memorial in Long Island. It is an Irish Catholic family funeral on a wintry February day. There are no photos of Luke at the church and no one mentions his beloved dog, or Saint Francis, or working the land, his queerness or his openhandedness (like when Luke's friend was dying and he took unpaid time off from the farm to sit with her for weeks in the hospital or the pans of eggplant Parmesan he would make for the crew). I am confused about the rules of this Catholic mass and burial. I didn't know it was allowed for someone who killed themselves. Luke would hate it and I discover, sitting in the pews, that he looked so much like his father. The priest sermonizes from a pedestal with three church ladies flanking him and holding cloth and communion cup. He stands above them, old and closer to death than Luke should have been. With practiced, unblinking pomp in the face of death, he recites memorized prayers in scrambled incantations. He speaks about the banquet with Christ, eternity, and spiritual joy. "Luke was made in God's image," he says. Luke spent some of his last weeks on this earth wandering and homeless with nothing. This is maybe how the saints got closer to faith.

Other times than these, life has miraculously flowed in the same direction as our will. On the carrot farm at harvesttime Luke and I packed row after row of carrots into milk crates, breaking off the green tops expediently as we went. We got so we could quickly top four or five carrots in hand before dropping the fistful into the crate. A wagon, piled with bin after bin, was intermittently pulled forward to keep pace with us. When I climbed atop the tractor and put it into first gear to move forward, someone shot up from the field waving their arms, so I punched the clutch down, stopping the fat tires of the attached wagon after they'd rolled a few feet. Luke's old dog, Sully, had been sleeping in the shade of the wagon wheel and the tire had rolled across his back before he could get away. Silently, he made a dignified limp out from beneath the trailer and we took him to the vet. Looking at the X-rays the vet said Sully was fine, though not untouched; actually the wheel had done some good chiropractic work on his arthritic hips. This gift was given to Luke because any other outcome would be too horrible.

But today there is a coffin and Luke is inside. It is closed, wooden, and held by the men of the family after being clouded over with incense, the thurible swung like a crane from the priest's old hand. The box looks small compared to life, almost like the coffin of a child. Luke was short and skinnier than he used to be. The pallbearers, somber in leather jackets, carry the coffin, draped in wreaths of yellow roses, outside. The waiting hearse's black doors are open to the cold and ugly daytime of the parking lot.

I don't go to Luke's mother's house for sandwiches afterwards. I can't face it. Instead Graham and I go to a nearby diner. Everyone there looks terrible. Maybe it is the pallor of the funeral cast out with cruel impersonality onto the diners, but they appear deathly with purplish skin and greasy hair moving against their jaws as they eat pickles and coleslaw and laugh in gulps of choked smokers' laughter. It all feels ruinous, me here in a vinyl booth and Luke just scratched off the earth.

From the table, now laid with coffee and sandwiches between Graham and me, I look over the tops of people's heads out the window to the bare trees and I think of the summer heat the day during my lunch break that I got a call telling me that an old classmate had overdosed. All afternoon I sat atop the tractor driving animals out of the field like usual, mowing down plants or digging up weeds to die in the sun. Knowing nature, it has become impossible for me to see death only on human terms.

There are things like unintentionally uprooting rabbits' nests, and orphaning the young of all types of animals, and then there is the task of understanding oneself as arbiter, raising an animal with designs for its death. Once I threw the heads of three pigs into a dumpster behind the VFW. My mother and her wife were in the car with me. The gas roared over the failing clutch as we laughed nervously at our sin, the impropriety of this burial. It was all that was left of meat pigs I'd raised that fall, kept in the cool garage for further foodstuffs until I saw flies leaving their mouths in drunken pairs. "Dirty deeds, done dirt cheap / Dirty deeds and they're done dirt cheap" played from the car stereo as we drove away, leaving the unattached heads there in the trash for some garbageman to find or truck to dump, unaware of the lives I'd reaped.

A woman in the diner, her booth nailed to the back of mine, talks to her tablemates about a friend who had a baby and something wasn't right; when she held it, it felt dead in her arms. She says this as they casually flip through a photo album one of them brought to lunch, slamming the pictures, page after page, on top of each other, annihilating what was. The plastic sound of the pages turning mixes with the clink of coffee cups. People, still very much alive, eat their soup and pie and suck soda through straws while the waitress snakes through the room from one table to the next, and in integers like this, time continues on.

I keep seeing death's face in different ways. It is funny to choose a profession, like farming, in which death is taken into the fold and yet nothing is clarified. It does not steady me for loss even if I have held a pig's head in my hand or seen a chicken collapsed in the dirt. It is like a blunting of the real. Life is cauterized and then the camera pans left onto that which still breathes, photosynthesizes, or sounds.

· Days of Harvest ·

XII

The Eve of Destruction

Summer 2019, New Lebanon, NY

The Lebanon Valley Speedway's annual Eve of Destruction begins with a truck balancing on its left side and lapping the track, an American flag waving from its bed. The singing of the national anthem opens the show and the clown MC, standing on a balustrade in center field, croons into a microphone, "Show me some love!" The clown's voice travels far from his person, little more than a far-off pair of bloomers and curly wig surrounded by dirt.

You can tell the women who are without kids at the speedway, not by age but by the way they work the audience, walking tall with a friend in tow along the fenced-in pit, so everyone in the amphitheater can look down at them. Women with kids have physical counterbalances pulling at the skin of their faces and breasts, the ends of their long hair. A mom sitting near me says to her son, "I couldn't pay someone to take you." His grandma on the other side of him keeps saying, "Quit shittin' around," and smiling at me and the other women sitting and drinking near her, so we may share in her adult admonitions.

It's summer again and I'm back in New Lebanon, returned to the vegetable farm, Graham and our other friends from town all packed against one another in the bleachers. Most of us work with our hands and though we carry a respectable layer of dirt, we still don't quite fit in. One friend, stinking of clove tick repellent, intermittently flicks on a sixteen-millimeter camera pointed at the track. We pass a cardboard box of cold beers between us, which we take turns descending the bleachers to refill, and sagging paper plates of fried dough and ketchup-smothered fries. We're pressed into the big crowd on what feels like a town holiday, but really people come from all over to watch. There are excited kids everywhere, packs of teenagers, generations of families, and couples on dates. We have all left our cars in the grass lot across the road, bought tickets from teenage attendants, visited the concession stand beneath the bleachers and the bathrooms with troughs for men and pink plywood stalls for women, and found our seats.

The first race features cars with their hoods and trunks popped up so the drivers can see only out of tiny cracks in front of and behind them. All the cars have girls' names spray-painted in hasty scrawl: HANNAH, OLIVIA, JENNAH. One just said PUSSY in jagged red letters. The cars get smashed and the hearts painted on bumpers crack up. Big chunks of metal and tires fly through the dirt. Kid Rock and Alice Cooper play through megaphones attached to the tops of fence posts surrounding the track. Between races, the clown says he's given away hundreds, maybe thousands, of bikes with his wife's help. He asks "anyone between the ages of five and ten who doesn't have a bike" in the audience to raise their hand and calls on a girl who looks like she's eight years old to come down to the center of the track. He gives her a bike and tells her, "There's no cryin' in learning to ride a bicycle," before saying to the rest of the kids, who didn't get a free bike, "Tell your dad to quit being cheap and go to Walmart and buy you a bicycle."

As the sun sets in metallic pink, a woman climbs the bleachers in a see-through jumper, holding the small hands of her little boys, one on each arm. Everyone notices, turning to look at her beauty, away from cars smashing into jumps and the drivers crawling out the mangled windows. She takes her seat on a sagging two-by-four, one of many arranged into the shape of an amphitheater. Two school buses standing on end are impaled head-on by a car. The attention is finally wrenched from her and people can't help but look back at the crunched-up cars, which rumble for their applause. The sound engulfs us all—each overpowered engine part of a static roar that suddenly changes pitch as vehicles fall away and break out into individual screams.

Two little girls in front of me shriek as the trailer event starts. Every race has a different set of rules with some new handicap to make it more treacherous. Trailers hitched to cars fishtail and fly around the ring, easily becoming airborne. In a parody of moving, some tow sofas. The best part is when the trailers fling into pieces and smash. A blue-and-white-checked couch flies apart, cushion by cushion, across the backstretch and cars plow through the mounting junk, blowing it to cotton balls and metal shards across their windshields. The little girls crack up at this, their tangled hair and food-stained T-shirts bumping against each other and hitting my knees. They turn back, say sorry, and ask me what my favorite monster truck is. "I like the dog with floppy ears that flap over jumps," I say. All of us agree though that the Green Mamba—the jet-engine-propelled car—is the best. When it laps the track, we can feel the heat of its flames against our cheeks.

In 2015, I came to the Eve of Destruction for the first time.

The gauntlet race that year began like any other, cars gaining speed. A pack of junk cars chased a striped Winnebago around and around the track, trying to hit the camper. The driver who wrecked it first would be crowned the winner. A black Jeep sped up and smashed into the RV, and instantly the RV collapsed. Its four walls fell neatly, one on top of the other, into a flat plane, trapping the driver. The motion began and ended in what seemed to be a matter of seconds.

After the crash, the clown announcer fell quiet and so did the audience: a bad sign. No music, no cars, no cheers. In stillness, dust clouds settled back onto the track and everyone waited. The emergency crews that stand by at all the speedway events quickly surrounded the flattened RV. Someone held up a big blue tarp in front of the scene so instead of seeing the driver dragged out from the wreck the audience just watched a wavering blue square under stadium lights, crudely censoring the accident. Maybe he was still alive then. The ambulance sped off the track and drove to Albany Medical Center, but the RV driver died from massive head trauma.

After the wrecked man was taken away, the clown came back on the loudspeaker, telling everyone to visit the concession stand while they waited for things to start up again. The show kept going. The towheaded farm kids were there that night; the youngest didn't understand the driver had died, but the older one did and asked his parents strange unprompted questions about how he died for days after. The driver's name was Shawn Rivers; he was an equipment and crane operator with five kids of his own. He worked on pipelines, dredging the Hudson River and building big bridges. His obituary stated he "died as he lived, fearless and fast. He rode motorcycles and snowmobiles to the limit, loved jacked-up diesel trucks and fast cars. He enjoyed the challenge of running equipment expertly."

A lot of people in the audience wanted the event to keep going. I felt guilty for having paid, after I knew for sure that Shawn Rivers died, like I'd helped hire his ruin. Afterwards, someone in town told me, unsurprised at what I'd seen, that people die what seems like every other year on this track.

It is not only cars that cause destruction. The last concert at the speedway was in 1980, after which the local paper ran the headline NEAR-RIOT (AND TWO CAR ACCIDENT DEATHS) AFTER THOUSANDS GATE-CRASHED A SHOW AT THE LEBANON VALLEY SPEEDWAY. Ronnie Dio was the lead singer for Black Sabbath on the Black and Blue tour, a double bill the band played with Blue Öyster Cult. From the concert video that I find, Dio appears smaller and more varmint-like than Ozzy Osbourne. Dio has a shock of frizzy hair atop a black-and-blue silk shirt open deep over his chest. The music pulses through Dio's five-foot-four frame in electric waves and flows out of his hands. Hands in fists, hands pointing, hands in devil horns (a gesture he says he learned from his Italian grandma), the guitar chugging behind him.

In the music there is the same kind of death wish, made into melodrama, found in the turns of the speedway, where the stage had been set up, flanked by two cartoonish white crosses laid on their sides.

Thousands of people came out that hot Friday night in August, many of them through the open field around the track. There were bikers and teenagers, drunk and on drugs: weed and acid and mushrooms and cheap beer; thousands of cold ones sold at the concession stand. Sweaty audience members fought to get up to the chain-link fence surrounding the band in the center of the track, or else were squashed against it by all the bodies in the crowd, only to be beaten back by roadies hitting people off with bats. People made fires, and someone carried in a thirty-foot cross painted black and lit that on fire too. It fell in a sweeping crash into the audience. There are pictures of concertgoers taken out with T-shirts wrapped around their bleeding heads.

In the video, Dio's face, bathed in red light, feels the power of the music first on one cheek, then when he turns his face and closes his black eyes, the other. He brushes his hands in soft psychedelic swirls beneath his long hair, conducting the electricity of it. The guitarist, Tony Iommi, in a tight leather jacket, flashes the whites of his eyes, the whites of his teeth, and the gleam of a cross around his neck. Dio is sweating through his hair and his dark shirt is slick as oil.

"A little white shape looked down at me, he said: heaven is where you ought to be."

Dio looks up into a white spotlight pouring over his face.

"He said, come with me, I know just what to do, but I said go away, I'm gonna burn in hell with all of you!" and Dio points to the audience in a big flowing arc, cracking a smile.

When Dio sings "Hell," he raises his right hand and clenches it in a fist over and over. Tony Iommi's eyes are half open and sweat falls from his temples in big drops. Dio and Iommi play back and forth to each other, with Dio grunting and Iommi riffing off it. Geezer Butler, the bass player, shakes his head back and forth, approvingly whipping his hair like a dog's ears. In an interview, Dio said "Heaven and Hell" was one of the best songs he ever wrote. "There are so many people out there who've got their hand in your pocket and their hand on your heart, and all they wanna do is take whatever you got to offer," he said. "Heaven and Hell" is what you have to go through to live in this world, the dark and the light, something the audience already knew.

Sabbath played fourteen songs, finishing with "Children of

the Grave." Blue Öyster Cult played fourteen too. Their set ended more gently, slipping into the suggestive guitar and whispering vocals of "(Don't Fear) The Reaper."

Five hours of vandalism and confusion followed the show. In the parking lot, fans flipped a car into the gully below. After smashing the windows in and pelting it with rocks and beer bottles, someone stuck a lit rag in the gas tank and the car exploded. Flames shot above the tree line and the whole grassy lot of passenger cars. A few cop cars approached the crowd only to be hit with rocks and drive away.

The guardrail just outside the lot was crumpled after a seventeen-year-old, Anthony Masdea, was struck by a drunk driver while trying to hitch a ride home. He lay there bleeding out, covered in a white sheet soaked red as the EMTs loaded him into an ambulance and thousands of cars full of screwed-up people crawled by, trying to drive home. Nineteen-year-old Brian Levesque died on the way home in a highway accident. All the deaths, on and around the speedway, were random, stupid even, but could be taken into the fold here, tallied alongside life taken by accident or by nature for no reason at all. Death courted and then shied away from. Conjured by all the races circling circling circling the track and the screams of Ronnie Dio. The concert prompted the town to get an injunction against rock shows, but the races are never canceled.

In the ring, drivers' lives contract and become as small as field mice before they are offered up to the track and extinguished. After Shawn Rivers died, I felt so guilty I didn't go back to the speedway that season, but the next year, when I did, a smile crept over my face as the first cars made contact and crashed together: it is *so* loud. The deafening drone of engines and low-lying smoke fogged the air, and the cheap beer pleasantly fogged my mind so that I felt good all over. Watching it is its own form of release. I like seeing things get smashed, and other people here do too. It feels like every anger could be avenged.

At the speedway, the violence is courted, at work it is unexpected. Accidents happen: hands are caught in balers; welds land hot metal on skin; people are sucked into their machines, fall from ladders, flip in forklifts; limbs are pinned beneath felled trees; cows' hooves collapse work boots. Mostly, the injuries are patched up and healed over. At the speedway, the violence that lies dormant in country life in the incessant harvest of big machines, plows cutting through earth, engines humming, and animals culled spills over into spectacle and is made palpable.

Beneath the functional job site lies a kind of prurient fantasy, perhaps born of the frustrations of manual labor or simply native to life itself, of destruction, for the familiar betrayals of machines, animals, and humans to come to a grinding apex. The desire for the planned to come up against the accidental, reactive, and uncertain nature of life is there in the bleachers of the speedway. For many of the audience members, private battles become part of the show, and the anger at the job, any job, the hours and the immutable tasks to be done is exorcised. Here we build a pyre to the effigy of work made in smashed machines and wrecked efficiency. Things that may never work again, things that will be hauled away and buried in a pit at the local dump and happily let go. The pieces, blown apart into their elemental ingredients of glass and metal, discover a newfound freedom.

Like so much around here, this racetrack used to be a farm. When the forest lay thick in the valley, Mohican agriculturalists burned off trees for plots of vegetables and pasture for wild game.

Later, early settlers felled whole swaths of birch and buried corn around the stumps, after which they would release herds of swine to dig around and uproot what was left. The stumps, unearthed by the strong noses of the pigs, were then pulled out by teams of oxen and a raw field remained. First the speedway was a subsistence farm, later it became one of the town's many dairies, all gone now, impossible to keep going with dairy farming's bad economics. The land is still in the family that kept cows here.

Maybe I like it here, in part, because the ruin of the old farm lingers. On farms I've worked at, when it doesn't rain I've seen whole plantings of crops fail or it rains too much and squash rots on the vine, tractors break in the field, livestock are stillborn, farmhands disappear. These attempts to facilitate the propagation of life flirt with its dissolution. The powerful machines and aggressively bred animals could be extensions of the thrum of the earth, the fragile animation of earthly things, or a kind of monstrous defect of it, a sick growth grafted onto the life we are given. Something that should be destroyed.

In this arena others died too. Though their deaths were accidental, I wonder if any of the drivers felt like Luke did when he decided he didn't want to live. Ron Zanolli, a double amputee—the result of a previous accident—was driving a hand-controlled race car when he left earth clocking in at 139 miles per hour. His parachute failed to open and Zanolli lost control, skidding six hundred feet before hitting a tree, soaring five feet above the ground. At twenty-eight, "Racin' Jason" Betwarda perished when he crashed his turbocharged Mustang against a barrier in a test run. Twenty-six-year-old motorcycle mechanic Jim Phibbs died flying off his motorcycle. He flew thirty-five feet from the track at an unknown speed. For an uncalculated moment he was free before hitting a parked station wagon.

Before Sabbath's last song of the night at the speedway, a strobe light flashed onstage. Blinding white light and all-consuming darkness alternated. On the video, with bells tinkling, Dio sings,

Die Young
Die Young Die Young
Die Young

XIII

Summer's Solstice

Summer 2019, New Lebanon, NY

Early in the season, I dream of snakes every night. They are big Floridian ones with black-scaled bodies, complex networks of them in the floors of houses or woven into tall grass. In the dreams, the snakes are potent, ominous even, but not altogether frightening.

In waking life, I find garter snakes in the tomato greenhouse, a maternal snake and her orange young the size of worms between hay bales, another society in a stack of old tires I move to mow the field, hoping I won't kill them with the brush hog. Instead I leave in my wake a frog on its back; its exposed belly and outstretched limbs shine death in the color white. I find a snakeskin peeking out from an old pipe in the ground near where the pig pen will go. The skin is only about a foot long and still perfect with little incandescent coverings where the eyes were and a natural curve that ended in the pointed tail. It must have crawled out the mouth hole, leaving its trace intact. I put it on my dashboard, but it blows out the window and slithers away from me down the road.

A wooden cross on a hill reads: JON "BIG COUNTRY" SAVIANO, the letters burnt into the wood. His obituary says he died at nineteen in a house fire with his dog here. A spotlight positioned beneath the cross points up at a Don't Tread on Me flag hanging from its arms so that the rattlesnake looks like it is undulating in the wind whenever I pass by. I scrape the bottom of my car on a ditch and drift off the road looking at it.

On the first day of summer, I get an eight-dollar haircut at Deb's Shear Perfection in town while Diesel, the pet pug of the shop, watches. The hairdresser, a head shorter than me, has me stand while she clips off the ends of my hair in a straight line. A lady getting her hair cut on the other side of the mirror from me says it is going to be a big snake year, that she's already seen a rattler and the summer's just begun. After ten minutes my haircut is done. I am shorn economically like a sheep and leave the shop as the woman in the salon chair continues her talk of snakes and ticks and the other creatures that bedevil us.

I drive past the grotto outside the Immaculate Conception church, to whose pantry the farm brings vegetables. Inside, the grotto holds a white plaster Virgin Mary surrounded by red votives blown out by the wind. The Virgin holds a rosary draped between impossibly white fingers. Bird poop dots her shoulders and water pools at her feet, fallen through the four rings of stone masoned around her like an earthy halo. Being a nonbeliever, I've never stopped to see her, but when I do I find a dead snake hanging in the cobwebs above her head in a hard black S.

I returned to Sarah and Ethan's vegetable farm in New Lebanon because I like the town for what it is: the sort of ugly strip of Route 20 it occupies bringing strangers who seldom stop, the small library, the Stewart's gas station, the Gallup Inn, the creeks and unfolding pasture, the warm Lebanon springs, my friends, the mountain—all of it still here.

Sometimes I want to quit farming. I grow tired of the people who work alongside me in the dirt, like we are all cheapened because of it. Reading a good book or hearing a good song in the morning, I don't want to go in, as if working itself were a failure of imagination for the weak or stupid. But as the season wanes, I forget, with the prospect of another job, the money it will bring, and the promise of a winter break to follow. Before spring even begins, seed catalogs with dog-eared corners pile up, waiting to be fulfilled and the pictures expressed into real leaves and roots. At the New Lebanon farm, we grow vegetables just because we like certain varieties, cultivating unpopularly bitter radicchios and giant pink tomatoes that split as they ripen alongside thousands of pounds of survival foods, rows and rows of potatoes and cabbage.

Working at the farm again, I notice some changes. People added to the crew, more acres cultivated, another old tractor in the fleet, the work truck blue now instead of white, and the barn has a concrete floor instead of dirt. But still, fundamentally, things are the same. The same low-slung Mount Lebanon and collective Shaker gravestone. The same weeds coming up in the fields, reseeded from so many generations. The same lunches of unwashed salad greens and boiled eggs at the picnic table beneath the locust tree. The road signs put up by the communards, one yellow diamond atop the other, still read: GOD'S CHILDREN AT PLAY and WAR IS A DEAD END.

I don't come back to the little yellow house. No one has lived there since Sarah and Ethan split up and moved to separate corners of town. This season, I live in a 1970s ranch home on a wooded road between other houses and forested lots overposted with Private Property signs and guarded by parked logging rigs. The house is set into a wall of new-growth woods strewn with TV parts, metal drums, and the original dwelling on the property, little more than a chimney and roof resting on the patchy grass. A stone wall runs through the woods from when this was all part of some bigger tract of farmland painstakingly cleared, sold off, and then given back to the inevitability of trees. In the front yard, a few apple trees are dwarfed by pines that hang above the one-level house. Inside there is a woodstove, linoleum brick-patterned floors, and lime-green walls. For years, I'd moved alone for the work season; this time, though, Graham moved with me. We share the house with our friend; her dog, Gugli; and our sister cats, long-haired Snowman and short-haired Valentine, for two hundred dollars each. The animals live free.

In New Lebanon, Graham's paintings become bigger and more green. The pictures are mosaic-like, filled with images of the ranch house, cats in the grass, the back of my head, ramps, the tree-lined road. One is a collection of local church steeples all pressed together as if they were an entire block ringed in clear blue sky. He painted the curtains in our bedroom to look like a Hogarth print—busy with caricatures of people on the street—to cover over the windows that look out only onto grass, tree boughs, and the occasional brown chicken. We visit the nearest museum over and over. He likes to look at the trompe l'oeils: a letter, a flower, a photograph tacked onto a cork board, their edges and petals curled in contrived three-dimensionality, looking more clearly illusory for it.

Sitting under cover from the sun in the Gallup Inn, I forget the horses cultivating potatoes, the tractors cultivating onions, threading twine between the tomato plants to get them to stand straight, weeding the beans and cilantro and inch-high rows of carrots, and lifting fence posts to mow away the groundhogs' undercover paths to our fields. I come to the bar to play Nirvana loud on the jukebox. I watch people make offtrack bets and cast the losing slips of paper into the trash cans waiting below the electronic betting machine. The TV changes from the blurred rush of horse racing to the blacks and blues of *Nightline* crime reporting. The bartender seems drunk and keeps leaving to smoke, her white-blond hair flying at its full-feathered wingspan in and out of the back door. It is nice to be back at the bar, stinking of tomato plants and drinking in the cool peace of the indoors; to be surrounded by artificial and manufactured objects, the lacquered tables and crunchy carpets asking nothing.

From the parking lot outside, I can see the white peeling house where Sarah lives now. The porch, covered in beach towels and inner tubes, obscures the shed she stays in behind the main building. She and Ethan are broken up more or less for good, and she continues to date women. A worry wrinkle has begun to show right between her eyebrows. Mine grow longways, instead, across my forehead. Neither Sarah nor Ethan considers quitting. After their fighting subsides, a silent animosity rests between them and translates to minimal contact. They work in parallel tracks at the farm, and Ethan spends long hours alone in the machine shop. Sometimes at the lunch table, Sarah pretends she can't hear him when he asks her a personal question. Her favorite things on the farm remain working the horses and planting flowers. She pores over seed catalogs, choosing varieties based on their ephemeral beauty. Some grow just tall enough to face-plant in the dirt and others are ravaged by mice. The bells of Ireland bloom elegantly into green conical flowers but are covered in well-camouflaged thorns that stick anyone who picks them. This year Sarah lets her hair grow long and shaggy and stops wearing a bra. Because she is so terrible with time and always losing it, she says farming is time therapy.

φ

Summer falls heavy and slow over everything. I start reading the
Farm Deacon's Journal, a farm ledger kept by the Center Shaker
Family in New Lebanon, written in ink whose color changes
from year to year, black to brown to blue, 1858 to '59, '60 to '61.

In June 1858 the Shakers wrote of how summer shuddered,

> *We realized a frost here last night, a very heavy frost. Lost
> almost everything . . . 2nd calf this spring*

and then gave way:

> *And now fair summer wreath*
> *Entwined with flower of ever shape & hue*
> *And the soft west wind breath*
> *The face of nature with gay life renew*
> *Farmers choring*

The Shakers' agricultural record hangs over the same plot of
land that I farm on now, though I am more like one of the hired
hands the Shakers called on for the apple harvest or haying season.
Workers who, even if they died on the job, were not counted
in the annual death tolls of the community of Believers. Being
celibate, the Shakers never had births to record, only the join-
ing of new members or the willful departure of Believers whose
leaving was often commemorated by the sentence "I don't think
you will see a great many wet eyes."

Amongst daily tasks and Sabbaths observed, I read in the ledger accounts of the misfortunes that befell the Shakers, misfortunes lodged in the repeating patterns of life on the farm and
more generally in any kind of life at all. The weather being a great
determinant of the success of their farms, the Shakers became
poets of it, its familiar scribe admonishing unrelenting heat or

rain, praising the beginnings of spring, and predicting the retaliations of the northern lights, "red as blood very brilliant. Storm approaching."

In the deep time of ripeness with farming money in the bank, I buy three piglets, young and unweaned, from a barnyard crawling with rats—rats frolicking in the sheep poop and amongst the hens and the other newborns of spring awkward and gangly now. Ten pounds each, the piglets are easy to grab from the litter, fighting for a pile of cracked corn, small and weak. Later I find they came with lice too. They are so little and wild that they easily escape the pen I set up for them in a field behind my ranch house. They slip beneath the zap of the electric fence and out into the brush, which envelopes their pink bodies except for the telling sway of grass above their heads. This happens a few times before they can be convinced to become my livestock. I feed them a combination of fetid farm vegetables, cafeteria leftovers, and bucketfuls of grain, though they also eat whatever wild things they can find. Roots dug up, snails, the nests of mice engulfed in their strong jaws. They eat and eat until they are overfed, and constantly there is the sound of their low-to-the-ground farts like pressure valves being released from their tightly packed bodies. In time, I name them and they take on three distinct sizes. Gudrun: small. Ursula: medium. Theresa: big. Instead of putting on fat, Gudrun wastes, becoming my skinniest pig yet. She looks like a pink dog. Her shoulder blades move like haunches as she rips apart a bread loaf like a mongrel. Her spine sticks out from her back, making her triangular in shape save for her protruding stomach, an unnatural polyp on her thin frame and the only part of her that is growing.

φ

The first big harvest on the farm is the chicken culling. In one day, we kill most of the sixty-odd layer hens, there to lay eggs for the commune to eat. The flock is three years old now and slowing down on laying. They often escape their fenced-in coop—a kind of chicken jalopy—and roam the farm, an ugly sight, tail feathers plucked red and raw and bodies thinned into bony caverns by the exertion of laying hundreds of eggs. We find them taking dust baths in the basil or senselessly cornered in the greenhouses on the hottest days of summer. Their ratty carriage has become like a bad omen, grizzled things on the farm not fitting the model of fresh and rapid production in which we abide. Now the chickens fall into the category of things to be plowed under or done away with. Because they are too tough to sell, we are working today unpaid, save for the filling of our own stew pots.

Graham, Ethan, and I do the killing, along with Sean, a new part-timer this year. When his family moved to town, Sean joined them from out West, returning in a gray pickup. He's just a teenager, really, and he's the only one on the crew who smokes cigarettes, whatever kind is cheapest, but since New York raised the legal smoking age to twenty-one, he has to go to a truck stop wearing a hard hat and walkie-talkie, so he doesn't get carded. He has a brother and sister, adopted into their family like him, who sometimes live with him. He grew up on Long Island, was bar mitzvahed there, and worked at a seafood restaurant shelling lobsters. He is handsome, with broad shoulders and raven-colored hair, and styles himself as a cowboy. He likes country music and lived out of a van for a while making a movie about wild horses. On the farm he weed-whacks all the fences. He is not good with hand weeding, finding the tiny plants to kill or save, because he can't focus—he just pounds holes in the dirt with his fist. He likes machines better.

Graham, without a full-time job yet, is here for the free

chicken. He doesn't care about farming really, which I mostly like about him, but he still lovingly cooks the vegetables we grow, melting down lard for greens, salting eggplant, and gently frying zucchini. He misses the city and reads oversized books about art and big novels (*Moby-Dick*) for a long time.

We trap the birds five at a time in a large dog cage and carry them, jostling inside so that the crate tips back and forth between our arms, over to the killing cones nailed to T-posts at waist height. The chickens are lifted upside down by their feet, one hand clamped around their flapping wings, their brown necks and red-combed heads gently threaded through the hole of the cone that holds their body in place. The birds hang swaddled with blood flowing to their heads. Sometimes they flap their wings against the metal cone or kick their yellow feet, but mostly they just hang there sedated by their own blood supply.

When each bird is dropped in a cone, I grab a thin neck with one hand and stretch it down into a long brown line. The chicken swallows and wheezes, fighting the constriction of its breathing tube before I drag my knife through layers of plumage into skin and maroon blood splashes out in a lifeful gurgle. The head comes clean off, falling into the sawdust poured over the grass below to soak up the blood of our flock. In the moment when the head hits, both head and body are still alive, with nerves or something else. From the pile of sawdust, the beak opens and the tongue reaches out, trying to call. The eyes open too, trying to see before the bird quiets. The body jerks, the wings wanting to flap but restricted by the cone. The feet kick.

One or two birds escape the cone, headless, flapping their wings and strutting through the grass. It is bad for them to flap wild like this because doing so could bruise the breast meat. Without a cone, I'd slit their throats with their bodies pressed between my legs to hold the wings down from wanting to fly.

Still hanging upside down, their cloacae open and close in pink paroxysms, feeling the outline of phantom eggs, but eventually all the birds fall quiet and the blood is drained away.

After their throats are cut, I lift the chickens by the feet, two in each hand, and drop them into a vat of boiling water. I stir the oversized pot with a stick, making sure to poke down the chickens' bodies, which keep floating to the surface, so as to scald them evenly. After a minute, once the scales of skin begin to slip away from the feet, I lift the chickens, sopping and hot, by their skinned, steaming white feet and place them into the chicken plucker. "Within thirty seconds your chicken should have their pajamas off," the manual says. The electrified plucker spins like a centrifuge lined with rubber teats that catch on the chickens' feathers, wings, and gangly legs, thrusting their inert bodies around in clumsy rotations until they are white and bare, coated only in the bumps where their feathers grew. The whole messy operation—the beheading, the water over a burner, and the plucker powered by an extension cord—is set up outside.

We take the chickens out of the plucker, newly naked. Old layers, not plump meat birds, they look thin with jagged breast-bones and compact legs tucked into their producing bodies. We eviscerate the birds on a large folding table. Death smells the same, animal to animal. Besides the more individual smells of pig shit or cow, there is a universal musk to it, and our aprons are coated in it, smeared in blood and bits of organ meat and the loose yolks of unlaid eggs. The chickens, being small animals, are easy for a human to pull apart. First an incision is made above the cloaca and it is traced entirely with a knife. Once the cloaca is cut around, a hand is slipped into the hole and the guts are tugged out. There are entrails, a little gallbladder, and a dark liver, which we separate and save in a metal bowl for liver pate. The stubborn lungs must be scraped from the ribs. There are whole rows of unlaid eggs, a line of tiny yellow yolks in the oviduct, some the size of Ping-Pong balls, covered in red veins, and a few fully formed in shells: the chicken's whole production line exposed.

At first, we forget to clean out their crops and have to go back and open the necks to find whole corn kernels, blades of grass, and little rocks for grinding up their stored food—it is always like this, the machine of the body interrupted by death, abrupt in its stoppage of production. In some crops there are broken-up shells from the eggs the birds have been cannibalizing in their coop. The carcasses, now empty of vitals and missing heads and feet, are dropped into a barrel of cold water to cool before being frozen. When we eviscerate them, they are steaming hot from the scalding. The living birds' temperature runs hot, around 106.

We let the Araucanas, the kind of chicken that lays blue eggs, live, and the rooster too. He is loose with a few dedicated hens and all of us are too wary of his sharp beak and pointed spurs to try to catch him. The rooster watches as we deplete his flock and allows it to happen. He never tries to attack us. Once all the birds are bagged and put into crates for the freezer, we begin hosing down feathers, blood, and guts from our tools. We gather the pile of chicken heads, drowning in rich red blood, and buckets of viscera, dump them into the tractor bucket, and drive it away to bury them in the digestive heat of the compost pile. I drive home with two fresh chickens in the back seat and Graham in the front with a bowl of livers in his lap, which he'll season and turn into pate that I'll refuse to eat—too close to the stink and heat of the birds from whence it came.

That night, I dream that the sister cats, Snowman and Valentine, and the three pigs are all together, with a big moose standing over them at the edge of a flowing river. It is a peaceful clearing in the woods, dark and deep, like in a Romantic painting. There is a strange sense of accord between species; the cats have shed the superiority that hangs around them in waking life as they watch the penned-in pigs. The pigs, neither wasting Gudrun nor fat Theresa, succumb to the frantic search for food, and the moose hangs like an insulating cloak around their shoulders.

There are no people in the dream.

XIV

Machine Work

Summer 2019, New Lebanon, NY

Some days in summer are spent alone with machines. Early in the season, before the corn and potatoes can be picked, and between the rains, when it is sunny and dry enough to cultivate, the tractor passes through immature onions, beans, peas, sunflowers, and corn, killing weeds with metal tines set in the ground and pulled, leaving rows of the desired crops and the weeds closest to them in green. The setup of the red tractors is all done with hand tools, wrenches and mallets used to loosen bolts and change out tines. There are hand cranks bolted to the floorboards because the tractors don't always start.

I rest my forehead against the steering wheel, pull the button to turn the machine on, and yank on the choke until it catches and the engine turns over. Raise the clutch too quickly before it warms up and the whole thing shudders and dies again. The shifter, too, requires finesse. A bald tennis ball serves as the knob to change between three gears, plus reverse. When the tractor starts, it releases a white puff of steam from its pipe, working out the residual moisture as I back out of the wooden overhang where it's parked, careful not to catch the tires on loose hoses and equipment piled around the sides of the shed. I push up the throttle a few notches and climb out of the machine shop drive with the façade of the barn sinking behind me.

I motor to the empty cornfield down the dirt road and a steep pull-off little more than a parting between tree trunks. In the morning it's still cool under their leaves. I park the tractor and unplug the electric fence before opening it and driving through. The field is quiet. I look for deer and woodchucks but see nothing. I drive midway to where the potatoes are planted, sprouted now into six-inch green solid plants. We use the finger weeders on them, spinning disks with rubber tines attached to gently uproot and smother the weeds around each plant. As the weeders spin in the dirt, fertilizer, from a plastic hopper balanced precariously on the right shoulder of the tractor, drops through a vacuum hose and onto the dirt beside the plants. The hopper emits a fine dust that blows around me as I drive. The tines behind the back wheels of the tractor dig into the dirt and clear the paths between rows.

I drive into the bed lined up so that the potatoes are centered below. With a lever, over and over, I drop the tines into the earth. The gears of the fertilizer hopper turn and the fertilizer falls. The finger weeders spin. I look with concentration at the plants as I pass over them. I drive staring below my feet, like being in a car with a hole in the floor, at potatoes as they flow by in wiggling lines that I follow, jabbing the thin steering wheel right then left, trying not to pull up the roots and the tubers of potatoes, no more than anemic-looking peas now. Always, a few die. At the end of the row, I quickly pull up the tines and drive a wide turn before pulling into the next bed.

The front tires are much thinner than the back so that when I hit a rock, it feels as if I'll tip before the tractor rights itself on the heavier back tires and keeps going. It is quiet enough that I don't wear headphones when I drive, but the engine becomes the only thing I hear, looking beneath the machine to make sure the plowing is working and in front to anticipate obstacles and try to stay straight. It runs slow, but keeping straight is harder than it looks as the light machine is pulled by the curves in the land and its natural obstacles. Even plowing up empty beds to plant the rows can become so crooked that I have to redo them all: a dip or swerve becoming accentuated with each added pass and eating into the next. Sometimes the small machine is maddeningly stupid, as is its operator. I drive a few feet before realizing one of the finger weeders has come off in the dirt somewhere, put the parking brake on with the engine running, and climb off to look for the weeder. I find it by the red paint and unnaturally black rubber dropped amidst loose dirt, walk back to the tractor, and jam it back onto its post before continuing.

I do the same thing row after row, stopping when the front wheels begin to spin in dirt as the back tines pin the tractor on a hill. It slides sideways, narrowly missing uprooting the rows of young potatoes below and on either side of the machine before I lift the tines out with a lever and right the tractor, sinking the tines back in again, more shallowly. It smells like dirt but also the sweet stink of fertilizer. When done, the potato patch is a more vivid brown. The dirt looks soft and crumbly between plants. I trick myself into thinking the weeds are gone, but soon another flush of thistle will emerge from invisible seed and poorly macerated roots all buried now in nicely turned over dirt.

I leave the field and break the shifter when I try to go into third gear. The shifter comes out of place so that the tractor does nothing but stall. I am now stranded by a patch of woods on the farm road, and all of the screws fastening the metal plate beneath the shifter must be unscrewed. Inside it is a color I have never seen. The working parts are an oil-soaked silvery blue, fishlike.

This is the only part of the tractor that is clean. The shifting column must be put back into its groove made of two C-shaped metal bolts that have to be pried back into alignment with an ill-fitting wrench from the toolbox beneath the tractor seat.

The afternoon is spent mowing on the blue eighties tractor. Unlike the older models, it starts reliably with the turn of a key and the press of a button. I switch between automatic gears and turn on the power takeoff, whose whirring revolutions set the attached mower's blade to turning in a loud crash. I pull the throttle up from a picture of a turtle to a hare and tow the mower behind me, cutting the grass from around the field, thus preventing it from growing into the cultivated rows (a different kind of fight against weeds than the careful cultivation). In between cutting long stripes in the field and tracing around parked tractor attachments, I watch for Belle and Lou. They are fourteen and fifteen now, though actually, we keep forgetting how old they are. Even though their life span is shorter than ours, they seem more like trees—bigger and slower than us. Belle is all brown, the dominant, opinionated horse. Lou, brown with a white-blond mane and colorless eyelashes, is the sweet, slow one. One day I found a bird's nest made purely from the hair of her mane, silvery white and woven into a strong bundle.

I drive the tractor over, plunge the bucket (controlled with a lever topped in the knot of a tree) into the rich soil, and fill the manure spreader that Ethan's driving with the horses. Compost fans out behind Ethan and the horse team in rich black spurts across the field.

The horses are like strangers to me, the night janitors. I see their good work, but know little of their natures. Lou is more yoked than Belle, and for that I identify with her. She's a hard worker but an economizing one. Some say she's lazy, but she'll run just to make it up a hill. She works with the inertia of a giant horse. Belle is more free, enough so that she forced her handler to stop while she smelled a lilac. She'll work but with stubborn fight. Lou's main defect is her itchiness, a violent itch will make her throw her fly-bitten body against a water tank, stable, or implement, rubbing her mane raw to get at it. If you reach beneath her greasy blond mane and scratch, her lips quiver.

I never learn to work the horses, since I know I won't keep my own. Instead I do hand and machine work, skills transferable from one farm to the next. Unlike the willfully skilled horses, the machines are of no mind. The barn swallows swirl around me on the tractor, coming close but never hitting my head. I try to count them, but they are diving and darting and tracing figure eights around each other like one great bird or a school of fish. They are here not to feed on plowed-up worms, cast-off seed, or fresh-cut grass but for the tractor. They threaten to perform their routine, to chase off a hawk circling too close before finally pecking at the bird's wings, undermining its easy glide with their own quick flapping. I see them, but quickly forget their empty threats as I look with concentration at the green. I turn off the mower after interrupting turkeys standing in tall grass and give the young a chance to escape. I turn the mower back on, scrutinizing wet clumps of grass and sod as I go for white bone or feather, afraid of accidentally chewing through a poult.

Sarah circles both Ethan and me on foot. She traces a slow perimeter weed-whacking the fence line, silver strands that hang between posts below the looming Mount Lebanon. When she runs out of fuel, we take a break and leave the field to get gas for the equipment. I drive the farm truck, which feels loose and quiet compared to the tractor. We listen to Top 40 and put our seat belts on before passing the cop who always sits in the same spot at the fire station.

The Stewart's gas station has moved across Route 20. All of

the Stewart's are moving from squat brick buildings to a new design that looks like a fake house with plastic siding. The old brick Stewart's are not destroyed but variously become liquor stores, auto parts shops, and food pantries. As a teenager, my mom scooped ice cream at one. Stewart's became big first as a dairy bar and second as a gas station that also serves as a kind of town mascot here, since there's nowhere else to get beer or gas. My mom had to wear a pleated skirt that would ride up and show her underwear when she bent into the freezer to scoop ice cream. Now the employees all wear baggy maroon T-shirts and visors, some with panic buttons on silver chains around their necks to press in an emergency.

Sarah and I pull into the pumps and I stand behind the truck bed filling gas cans on the pavement while watching a man walk across the lot. I notice him first for his feet, shoved inside tiny black cowboy boots so it looks like he's balanced on hooves. Scanning upward I see that he has scraggly shoulder-length hair; he's a billy goat of a man. I go inside the gas station behind him and he orders an iced coffee while I fill paper cups with hot coffee from the carafe. He leaves the store and clops back toward his truck holding his cold coffee. He pulls the handle on the driver's side door and it pops out flashing the words LUCIFER FARMS in an arch of black letters on its side. He climbs up into the seat and pulls the door shut so that the text flashes from one position to the other LUCIFER FARMS LUCIFER FARMS. Sarah sees it too.

We drive back out to the field with only an hour and a half left of work. Sarah pours more gas mix into the weed whacker, puts her face shield back on, lowering mesh over blue eyes and dark sweaty hair, and jerks the pull cord, starting up the motor again. I get back onto the blue tractor, hot from being parked in the sun, and turn on the mower. Ethan paces the field with the horses before dropping the manure spreading and leading the team up the hill and out to graze, sweat-stained from their harnesses. Time passes quickly under the hum of machines. The mowing isn't finished and neither is the fence line. Both are abandoned to work for the next day, which feels both as if it will never come and that it is already starting, hanging around us even as we go home at night.

In the brush behind the ranch house, the pigs' good-natured veneer quickly thins to expose their bad health. Inside, their ears are filled with brown plaque; outside, red bites. Their eyelashes look wet, alternately soft with mucus or stiff with goop; under their eyes is permanently smeared in dark stains from the runoff. They cough in hoarse waves, beginning in the ribs and traveling up and out of their bodies. The three of them rattle their thick heads, trying to get at the plaque in their ears, creating loud flapping noises, or else, in an attempt to correct some imbalance, they simply tilt their heads and hold them to the side in stiff discomfort.

Soon there is a brown bottle of penicillin in the refrigerator and syringes in the cabinet. We leave the medicine on the counter until it is room temperature and then fill the syringes with tiny amounts of pink liquid for the pigs.

"Ready?" I ask, trying to hold each small and quick-necked animal steady while Graham takes the needle and jabs it in behind the oversized pink ears. First there is a squeal of acknowledgment, then a pearl of blood from where the needle goes in. "The skinny one, she needs it most," I say, and Gudrun is stuck too, only to return to her grain bowl after the initial surprise of it. It makes me love them more, this dedication to the singular goal of eating. They are not vengeful animals, they come with simple preferences. After the penicillin, and before the deworming is complete, the pigs are doused in insecticide for the lice that bite them. The calendar becomes marked with the days of treatment, when cycles begin and when they should conclude. This batch of pigs must be nursed like no others, who seem to have slipped easily into my hands and then out again when they were right for eating. A hunter once told me they didn't like getting turkeys because most of them are covered in lice, something you don't realize until after you've shot one. I wonder if more of the natural world is like this than I knew.

Every morning on the farm, the crew convenes in a patch of sunshine around a clipboard covered in lists of work to be done for the week. Otherwise things will be forgotten: deliveries will be missed, plantings will not be done, the weeds and vegetables will go unpicked and grow monstrous or spoil. We have two new hands, Kate and Jess. Both moved here to work on the farm and live at the dead end of the road in old Shaker buildings for seasons on end. As we talk, Ethan hurriedly scrawls tasks and crosses off what has been done while his small black dog watches him with submissive devotion, his familiar pink lips and brown near-mulletted hair.

Usually, there are five of us. We fill the truck bed with empty crates and pile into the red cab, stirring up dirt from the cushions covered with crumpled-up clothing. Cast-off jars of drinking water roll beneath the seats. Half-rotten tomatoes and hot peppers, saved for some unusual quality and forgotten, bake on the dashboard. The dog presses against the passengers and thrusts her shining black head out the window, sniffing the air as the truck rolls slowly down the road to the field. When we get to the fence, the brakes come to a slow shuddering stop before Kate climbs out of the cab to open the gate. She strains for the top handle of the fence with her swollen hand dotted with poison ivy.

Kate spends part of the week working in the pentacle-shaped herb garden at the commune. At home, she and her boyfriend keep their own garden of strange healing plants, whose blooms she picks and roots she digs to make tinctures for immune support and aphrodisiacs. She comes to work in a beat-up Camry and for lunch always brings a can of kippers or sardines hanging in a basket from her elbow. She works out after our hard days on the farm and her work jeans fit tight against her strong thighs. The farmer we buy hay from is always trying to set her up with his son. The rest of us seem too strange. She is the only one of us with the patience to organize the filing cabinets and answer the farm voicemails. She feeds off this kind of work, her eyes grow wide in excitement. Her sister's a farmer too, a similar-looking redheaded Italian with thousands of animals under her care "if you count the chickens," Kate tells me.

As four of us drive into the squash patch to pick, with the loose side panels clanking against the truck bed, Jess spots a huge woodchuck in the unmowed grass. Sarah, Kate, and I scream for her to accelerate, and she does. Leaning forward in the seat so her foot can jam on the gas, she rolls over the woodchuck with a fatty thump, then reverses and hits it again. The same fleshy contact is made between tire and blubbery hide. Screaming girlishly, all of us get out of the truck. "It's not breathing," I say, looking at it cautiously. Now it is just a mound of brindled fur and four stubby paws, its small black eyes open and unblinking. The woodchuck is on its back and its rodent incisors protrude from its slack mouth, inside which a green bite of our lettuce is trapped. It was already fattening for winter, able to consume a pound of plants in daily forage on the farm—for this feasting woodchuck's teeth, like those of beavers, never stop growing.

This death was different than when we smoke-bomb the woodchucks' holes and leave them buried in networks of burrows beneath the farm to die. I still don't want to pick up this woodchuck, thinking it will snap back to life and its curved teeth and prehensile claws will be used against me though its strength lies more in accumulated fat than anything else. The surprised groundhogs that get away look like flying carpets in reds or browns. When they flee the vegetables they've been eating, their thick hides undulate in an almost watery motion, floating atop four paws until they disappear into one of their holes.

Jess came to the farm last year from Indiana, regretfully leaving behind her whole extended family. She came in a school bus, before it was broken down by mice chewing through wires, with a boyfriend (which didn't last either). She fell in love with Ben, the cook turned handyman at the commune, and moved into his house with the pit bull and big furnace of a woodstove right in the center. The two of them look like cherubs, blond-haired with rosy cheeks but hard calloused hands. She is the smallest of us on the nearly all-female crew. When we go swimming together in the pond, her long blond-green hair falls over her slight taut body that's like a stick with the bark peeled away, and her muscles pop from her arms, the ornaments of her work. She has a good mind for farming, understands how to plan a farm and execute it.

I'm not surprised that, seized with protective adrenaline, she'd kill a woodchuck and only later be overcome with Catholic guilt for her instinctual fury. We work together side by side five days a week, joking that we are like an interchangeable farmer, each performing the same tasks, driving the tractor over the same beds. Sometimes when we transplant together, we work in perfect unison, our arms like pistons on the same machine. I grow very fond of her.

I wait until after five to go back and find where the wood-chuck remains. I wrap its brown back paws in burdock leaves and carry the stiffened body through the fence wire to fling into a field of goldenrod just starting to bloom. It lands with a pregnant thud in a bed of flowers.

XV

Fairgrounds

Summer 2019, New Lebanon, NY

After work we go to the county fair. I buy a strawberry ice cream from the Mennonite girls in long dresses and sneakers, and Sarah gets a butter-soaked baked potato before we head to the show ring and watch the hog competition. Sarah sits with her potato propped on her legs, eating with a plastic fork as she watches. An old dairy farmer in the bleachers tells me the pig showing is much calmer now than it used to be, pigs being territorial animals. Integrating new pigs into a herd is best done in the dark of night. Some people douse the pigs in vinegar so they can't differentiate between their familiars' smell and that of the unknown.

The announcer says into the microphone, "For those of you who thought you didn't like pigs, they are pretty neat." She tells of pet pigs and pumpkin-eating pigs, how they designate a bathroom in confinement and the simple anatomical fact that they can't sweat. Sawdust catches in the sunlight as preteens in western wear carry little crops behind their animals, and large men in cutoff T-shirts hold hog panels to try to direct them. The contest is to reward good breeding and to teach kids about animal husbandry. The kids, some with more porcine faces than others, tap the rumps and shoulders of their pigs to direct them around the show ring while carrying soft-bristled brushes to arrange their pigs' nearly bald hides. The young handlers walk in measured steps, bringing an air of clumsy decorum to the ring, while the pigs trot semi-obedient zigzags before them in a flimsy agreement of docility. One barrow is covered in red scratches but wins his category anyway. Two prepubescent sisters in Coke-bottle glasses and blond French braids circle the ring behind their Berkshire crosses. Their cowboy boots and tight bell-bottom jeans flash behind the four-legged black-and-white pigs, nicely proportioned without the overgrown shoulders and low-hanging bacon bellies of the others. They are more dignified *animal* than a mere aggregation of ideal cuts. An old man sitting on the same bleacher I am, in pressed blue jeans with hearing aids tucked behind his ears, lets his eyes rest over each animal.

Pigs are funneled in and out of a gate to the barn to compete in different categories. One pig, weighing in at 258 pounds, froths at the mouth, overheating before finally refusing to walk at all, but he wins the Grand Championship regardless before being taken back to his pen to be watered. The scratched and bothered animal descended from a species 40 million years old, as opposed to his handler, whose ancestry dates back only about 6 million. "The family tree of the pig overshadows that of Adam and Eve like a giant redwood shading a mushroom," one pig historian wrote. The boy with the winning pig is given a huge purple-tasseled ribbon that he will staple to the barn wall above where the pig stays for the duration of the fair to be looked at before going back to the farm. To complete the cycle of rearing, training, and showing, many of the pigs will be sold at livestock auction.

Hanging around the pig pens afterwards, an oversized farmer in coveralls tells me the kids practice walking their pigs down the shoulder of the road. Even with the threats of the occasional car, or alluring foodstuff on the roadside, pigs like the open road and will trot along with feigned obedience under the tutelage of their handlers. In the whole competition there is this ideal of training; the kids try to emulate the gravity of adults in the ring while the pigs remain semi-oblivious to the show and their ultimate fates. For a long time, farmers lacking the wherewithal to pen them in kept their pigs in a semi-husbanded state between domesticated and wild, allowed to roam until they were culled for eating.

Outside the show ring, everywhere at the fair I see pregnant women. Pregnant women selling buckets of fries, watching their boyfriends wreck in demo derby cars, and eating baked potatoes in the exhibit hall. Even from the top of the Ferris wheel I see them, walking with their centers of gravity distinct from those of the rest of the population. I sit next to Graham, in a sweaty green T-shirt, his brown hair and brown summer beard cut short. When we are chained into a toy gondola, his shoulders rest nearly a foot above mine. As we slowly rise to the top of the wheel, we're laughing at the fun of hovering over the fairgrounds in bright-lit style. He flashes me his front teeth, slightly crooked, pointed toward each other instead of away. I never think we'll break up even though people break up all the time. Our gondola pauses at the top of the Ferris wheel so we can see the smoke rising from the demo derby and the lights from the games—shoot the bottle, win a goldfish—and the cotton candy and fried dough stands pouring out smoking fry oil and music.

Despite the easy warmth of summer, Gudrun's fur begins to grow in thick, a sign of starvation. She's not getting better. Over the phone the vet says it sounds like bad genetics, "poor thrift." She had a chicken like that once, just wasted away for no discernible reason.

"Don't get fat," Graham says into the pig pen when he is alone, not wanting them to die by our hands.

Soon, Theresa takes on the exaggerated shape of a pig. Already she and Ursula have lost their fey piglet natures and become feed-conversion animals. Fifty-pound tanks that traverse the pen sucking up food. Gudrun chases the squash that roll through the dusty pen; light and jumpy, she is an inverse cartoon of her sisters' piggishness. They bark when approached, owning their little plot of fenced-in land and holding their noses up for the scent of compost. Gudrun and Theresa don't have gray eyes like some pigs but big brown ones, with glossy irises that cast warm looks through dark lashes. Ursula wears symmetrical black splotches below each ear like barrettes. Beneath the splotches one eye is brown, the other blue. A single blue eye is rumored to be the mark of a good mother in a pig. At first I think the blue eye might be blind and wave my hand slowly before Ursula, occluding each eye in turn. She senses the movement equally in both eyes, turning her head in acknowledgment.

Overwhelmed by plentitude, the sisters circle one another to check what each is eating, to see if one has found the finest bite and to steal it. Gudrun, being the smallest, is especially susceptible to theft. The best tomato is easily taken in a single hard shove from Theresa. Watching for it, I do not see Gudrun's natural conviction to eat flagged by weakness. But Theresa wildly surpasses Gudrun's diminished frame, a blunt pink refutation.

A month passes and Gudrun stays skinny. Her tailbone protrudes in a taut line between her narrow hips to the sudden end of her clipped tail. When it is still dewy darkish morning, I scare the pigs, walking soft on wet grass toward their pen. The points of ears and the blacks of eyes pivot in my direction. *Ruff-ruff-ruff!* Ursula and Theresa answer. Gudrun, shocked, falls into the grain bowl, her legs splayed. When she recovers, Gudrun eats heartily, her hip bones pointing out like hames. I will continue to care for her, and if she dies, I will bury her far enough away from the pig pen that her sisters don't dig her up. It is easy to forget the abject place of pigs. They seem right, good even, with their ease of purpose fulfilled. When ill the pig reminds of all its banishments, somehow survived to be in these woods.

There is a potluck dinner at the farm with tables set up outside next to the field of garlic. Our CSA members come, and so do people who live on the farm road, some of whom grew up here, though mostly they moved for the commune decades ago. The tree-lined road is dotted with gray-haired Sufis in homemade houses, some octagonal, others with sugar shacks or saunas connected by strands of prayer flags. I sit at a picnic table across from a woman who used to farm here thirty years ago. She's brought a cold cucumber buttermilk soup to eat (Sarah and I brought a bad, half-cooked zucchini casserole we made at her house in the rushed minutes between work and dinnertime).

We talk of the vegetables of the field and discover we both have a fondness for celeriac, one of the undersung vegetables, and the big blue New Holland tractor. We both like bears too, and she watches them in her yard. I tell her about the bats and hummingbirds I see at my house, that there's more in the sky than on the ground. She tells me red-tailed hawks used to eat the rats right out of the compost pile here.

But that was years ago, now she's old. She works for the town library. She wears a wig that looks like a flake of hay. In a picture I saw of the farm crew from the eighties, they are all young, svelte from hard work, and dressed up in funny clothes, their bodies proudly draped across the tractor as if it is a prize—the new implement that they could afford to buy. I find the farmers' ledger from those days in the barn filing cabinet. It is made up mostly of sheets of purchases and sales, things canned or sold, hits sustained. The cost of seed is chronicled, soil tests recorded, hay bought in, and in a miscellaneous column one year someone wrote "Foot injury $22." In the 1987 harvest record, a note reads, *Food lost to bad methodology sauerkraut dumped + relishes + catsup. ⅓ winter squash rots due to temp. and humidity.*

Suggestions for 1987: *Grow more lettuce, spinach, Brussel sprouts, red cabbage, carrots, herbs-sage-basil-dill, flowers, summer squash, fall broccoli, beets.*

In 1989, someone reflectively wrote, *We sold more produce this season than any in the last 4 years . . . the small fry doesn't make it. It would be to our advantage to come up with a guaranteed crop . . . They've [the local grocery] been nice to buy our excess but it's not the real professional mode.*

From an 8:30 Monday morning meeting, ⋆ *problem—labor morale—efficiency. We need to work harder. We have an immense amount of weeding to keep up with planting and integrating. The entire farm is flagging as we fall behind.*

A message in thin black ink across the neatly gridded book of accounts reads, *I gave up this year, discouraged, feeling unsupported by the Sufi Order. I neglected the farm to go to battle over community issues . . . Very difficult times—heart breaking.*

Now the farmer turned librarian prefers to spend her free time with the animals. She feeds the deer cracked corn on snow in her backyard; they've come back to her for generations, she says, smiling, and sinks her dentures into her corn on the cob before ladling more cucumber soup into her mouth. She fed the raccoons too, a three-legged mother and multiple generations of kits, until they became too comfortable coming and going inside her house and pantry.

We both agree that deer are better than people. Even if they eat our vegetables from the field before we can get to them ourselves. She flashes me a corn-filled smile when I suggest this. "There are so many of them," she says, "but there are *so, so* many people!"

After we finish eating and leave the table, I watch her unwrap an ice cream sandwich and talk to a dog at her feet as if it were a person.

Guardian Angels

Autumn 2019, New Lebanon, NY

August falls to September and the nights and mornings have already become cooler. The sun sets earlier on the pigs' mud pit and goldenrod-filled pen, which has begun to sour, sounding the call for fresh pasture. On a Saturday evening I feed them soft cucumbers and slashed zucchinis. This year the bumper crop is cucumbers. Towers of boxed cucumbers crowd the farm cooler and amount to more than we can sell, eat, or can. The pigs have the same red bug bites on their ears as my cats. All of the animals itch them blankly, getting at something that will never be fully attained. When I come into the pen the pigs rub their thick skulls against my pant leg trying to get deeper into the itch. They brush harder and harder so that I have to push them off or fall into the pen with them. Sometimes the draft horses try to run away just to scratch an itch.

After work we go to the Gallup Inn. People at the bar are talking about how their winter squash turned out this year and the Yankees are playing on the muted TV. On a green chalkboard next to the TV, the bartender has written: ONE EAR OF CORN CONTAINS HOW MANY KERNELS? in white chalk. Sarah walks from her house across the dirt lot with her friend, carrying a big tray of buffalo chicken dip to the bar. Her friend puts Bachman-Turner Overdrive on the jukebox. Afterwards I put on "School" by Nirvana, which a big guy at the bar likes, and "Tops" by the Rolling Stones. Ethan drives over. We order beer and gin and tonics and play pool, Sarah and Ethan on opposing teams. I sit in the same chair at a table for hours. The night passes: seven to eight, eight to nine, nine to ten. I pay another dollar to hear a Deep Purple song on the jukebox. A woman at the bar asks what I do and I tell her about the pigs and the farm. "I love pigs!" she says.

"Me too."

"I have five of 'em tattooed on me," she tells me, tapping her ankle to say, One here, where her skin is covered by jeans. "They're my special pigs. They all have wings."

The bartender sets down my three beers and I say good night before I learn what the pigs are for. Guardian angels, maybe. Early man did not have much use, or evidence, for the belief that people and animals were distinct from one another. Bears could speak, but they chose to be silent. When animals were killed, hunters would ask them to return, to be killed yet again. The pigs beneath the woman's jeans are suspended, waiting to return, or maybe they are meant to represent people, lend their image of the fatted pig to cover over the more vulnerable human one.

I carry the beers to our table and turn to go to the bathroom. Outside the entrance is a Looking for Love poster written in pen and xeroxed with real photos carefully cut out and taped to it in a collage of personal totems. One is of the poster's author shooting a crossbow. Another is of her trailer in winter and fall to show the different seasons she lives in. And there are pictures of a mouse, a black bear, and a moose to show the wildlife. "Looking for a country white," the poster says, to eventually move onto her family's plot of land with her. She likes cooking, hiking, gardening, fishing, and camping. You need not like all those things, just some. Most important, you can't be lazy. I put my fingers around the edges of the moose picture, rip it off, and put it in my pocket because I want it and the country white part makes me sad, that she wrote that while also using something as humble as a field mouse to represent herself in some way. I come back to our table with the picture in my jeans and there is hardly anyone left at the bar. We buy another round of beer, but soon it's time to leave so the bartender can close up—you can't really stay anywhere late here.

I tack the picture of the moose—its massive, awkward body surrounded in the green fringe of summer grass—over my writing desk. It's not just the picture but something in it connected to the loneliness here—words, signs, talk at the bar between strangers all projected out from that point.

With all the ephemeral leafy vegetables and fruits ripe and heavy on the farm at once—the soil turned to cantaloupes, corn, tomatoes, and lettuces—we begin to dig the root crops from the ground. Ethan bought the farm a hundred-year-old potato digger from an equipment yard in Pennsylvania that is the size of two football fields. The guy who sold it to him drew a map of Amish country so Ethan could drive through and look at all the farms. There were no power lines, but the longest clotheslines he had ever seen. On the porches, there were daughters in the same color dresses and out in the field sons cutting down corn row by row with horses.

We haul the heavy digger on a wagon out to the potato field, where Ethan hitches it to Belle and Lou. The digger's clanking gears connect to a plow set deep in the ground to slash it open and reveal rows of potatoes sowed in spring and multiplied now.

Uprooted, they are scooped by the blade onto a circulating conveyor belt, where they are shaken free of dirt and deposited back into the upturned earth in a neat line for us to gather in buckets, crawling through the rows behind the horses. Belle and Lou fight bitterly through the harvest. It is hard to sink the heavy blade into the earth and pull it apart. At the beginning of each bed, they strain against the closed surface of the ground. Lou bites at Belle's thick neck when she refuses to pull her share. They both violently shake off horseflies that bite through their tough hides dotted, now, with blood and insect wings. Perhaps they don't like the unfamiliar machine, with its clanking gears and obstinate force, this aged seam ripper they are goaded to lap over the field back and forth all afternoon, continuing the struggle of many horse teams before them. Once I dreamt that there were only two pupils left at the elementary school, and subsequently they were forced to become resolute companions. The dream, I think, was about the horses never parting yet arbitrarily paired.

Before 12:30 we collect the dug potatoes into buckets and Sarah finds a nest of mice, pink and fetal, next to their mother, dead under the blade of the potato digger. Sarah, Kate, Jess, Ethan, and I pile into the red work truck and drive down the road to the barn. Sean drives his own truck between fields, I think because he's paranoid about being stuck out there. From the cooler in the barn, a black bin of lunch stuffs is produced: heads of dirty lettuce; jars of pickles, mayonnaise, and relish; oil and vinegar; and boiled eggs. We gather bowls and forks from the sink, ripe tomatoes and a loaf of bread from the "farm store," the profitability of which our hunger continues to undermine.

We carry everything over the little footbridge crossing the creek to a picnic table beneath a locust tree. The fragile leaves fall off unseasonably early and we are left missing their shade, which we like to sit in at lunch, letting our heads rest from the sun, its heat having been steadily on us the five hours before break. The crate of food unloaded, we each take a knife and fork and begin cutting up lettuce and spreading mayonnaise in layers across slices of bread. Kate and Sarah share a can of tuna or sardines almost every day. Ethan delicately cuts his vegetables and mixes them with bread and mayonnaise into a kind of chopped salad gruel, which he thoughtfully prepares well after everyone else has begun eating. I make sloppy sandwiches with thick-cut tomatoes. Jess crafts desserts out of the dollar-store peanut butter and marshmallow bought to bait mousetraps in the barn with. We eat with unfettered hunger; the yolks of eggs run together with salad dressing and tomato juice and drip down our shining chins. We pause only to slurp intermittently from a collective water jug.

At first, especially before he gets his paycheck, Sean tries to eat the same farm lunches as we do (plus cigarettes, which he smokes away from the lunch table in white puffs drifting above his black hair). Not liking plain vegetables much after running machines for hours, he switches to buying bacon-chicken-ranch pizzas from the diner in town. For whole minutes, there is only the sound of chewing at the picnic table. But usually at lunch everyone is happiest talking of things forgotten nearly as soon as they are uttered. We don't talk of the afternoon's work waiting for us. On the hottest days, the table grows quiet. When we are done eating, Ethan's black dog is given the empty can of fish to lick.

After lunch we return to the potato field to continue digging. The baby mice are still breathing, but lining their nest, exposed to the hot sun, they will soon die. It is grotesque, their undone home, but they would only grow to devour the field of carrots next to where they've been birthed, chewing down the tops and bringing rot to the field. Always, we choose our own stores against theirs.

Bucket after bucket of potatoes is hauled to the wagon, and

the horses continue to drive the digger, their hides wetted in
dark brown streaks. When they are resting at the end of a row,
they decide to trot away with the unwieldy digger still harnessed
behind them. The trot turns to a jog and the digger bounces
wildly behind Belle's and Lou's heavy hooves so that Ethan has to
run in a diagonal through the potato field to grab the reins. Once
regained into service, they continue to nibble at each other's
shoulders.

As we unload fifty-pound sacks of newly harvested potatoes
into the barn, a man sick with cancer of the blood shows up to
buy garlic in his beet-red Buick, so low to the ground the bottom
nearly scrapes against the gravel drive. He comes every year, so we
know him now as Garlic John because he says eating garlic will
help cure him. He came to buy one hundred heads and seeing
how nice it looks decides on the spot to get fifty more. He eats
a raw clove every day, he says. His black hair is combed across his
balding head and from beneath an inky mustache he talks to me
through mostly broken or rotted teeth. He asks me,

"Aren't you guys Muslim?"

"No," I say, "the Sufis kind of are, this is their land."

"But, is Ethan Muslim?"

"No."

Then he asks me if we're all *together*.

"Ethan got so many pretty girls workin' for him. I mean do
you all live on his commune?"

"No, we all live separately."

"But you've come from all over to be here. Indiana, Massachusetts, Vermont," he says, reading our license plates from the
lot.

Is it something strange about the mountain? I wonder.

At the Gallup Inn, they say people dance up here naked.
Once, someone called Child Protective Services, worried about

children being raised in a nudist colony. Or is it something off about the garlic eater, or the simple fact of working women? Even though I know the rumors about the commune aren't true, I don't want the townspeople to think I live here, that I'm one of *them*. I just come here to work. The commune itself used to be full of work: there was a bakery that sold its bread in town, an auto shop over the border in Pittsfield, they made ice cream to sell, there was a school for kids on and off the commune, and a nature center. All of these various operations are ceased now. The commune began some forty years ago, at a time when communes were multiplying across the country. Like the others', its membership swelled and then dropped off. People realized how hard it was to live together, or maybe they just didn't believe anymore. There used to be some two hundred people living on the mountain. Before Graham found work, the commune hired him to paint houses and then to dig holes for signposts and help cut down trees. I'd drive past him on the tractor or in the truck while he was perched on a ladder or buried waist-deep in a hole. He soon found another job, hanging art.

Garlic John pays me two hundred dollars for the garlic and climbs back into his aged Buick. I put the money into the small wooden cashbox next to a refrigerator of eggs and pickled vegetables for sale in the barn.

I return home from the potato harvest ravenous, and after dinner I sink like a stone. In the night, I wake Graham up, poking him hard through his T-shirt to tell him seriously, "We have to get the rest of these potatoes out." The next night I dream I'm driving the old 1950s tractor through the snow, that I'm back in Vermont and my clutching foot is freezing in soaked-through tennis shoes. Thoughts and dreams all circulate through a vocabulary of the farm as work climaxes into the fall harvest.

The next day, when I go to count the farm store money for

deposit, it's gone. This is the second time this year the farm's been robbed, and now I just feel stupid. All that's left is three quarters and two dimes. I don't really want to know who took it. The Shakers, accepting the inevitability of theft, used to plant extra crops to satisfy the thieves and the crows alike.

XVII

Fattening

Autumn 2019, New Lebanon, NY

It is the second half of September and still warm enough to jump in the pond, whose surface is covered in green duckweed that catches in our hair and sticks to our skin when we swim naked on our lunch break. The harvests come in giant batches now. The farm is picked through crop by crop, turning whole fields back to naked dirt. The onions are harvested after their tops have died back, and all the winter squash is cut from the vine.

At the Gallup Inn, a woman leans back on her barstool and says she found giant worms in her basil. "Horrible, scared the shit outta me!"

Graham and I sit at a table between the jukebox and the pool table. On our second beer Graham says he doesn't like keeping pigs so close to our house.

"It's fucking disturbing. I'm sick of all the animals."

I make machine-gun noises, shooting my finger over the table execution style. "Why?" I ask. I like it, all of us close.

We finish our beers and I walk in a diagonal across the dirt lot to Family Dollar to buy Ziploc bags to hold a fecal sample from

Gudrun. The woman on line in front of me slams a pack of boxers on the counter, saying, "I'm sick of looking at his holey ass."

For thirty dollars I can get Gudrun's poop analyzed in the vet's lab to see if she has worms. I feed the pigs the last of the cantaloupe, bitten into by bugs and mice. I stomp the fruit open with my boots so that the orange melons spill out and the pigs bury their snouts into the cool flesh, pink snouts and orange fruit engulfing one another in turns. Sometimes when they feed it is disgusting, but today it is with a profound sensual enjoyment, their tactile noses reverently roaming the innards of the sweet fruits. I sit on a log in the pen with the bag in my pocket, waiting for Gudrun to poop, watching her frenzied search for bits of overlooked food, too concerned to shit. Gudrun has grown, but only taller. She is preternaturally fast-running and hairy like a calf, a strange and half-starved creature, part of her porcine identity lost to sickness. Theresa grows more tanklike and has taken on the stilted movements of a fat animal. She picks up a fallen stick, trotting it through the pen like the grand marshal of a parade, before all three sisters begin to chase one another in wild rings.

I leave the unfilled Ziploc bag on the top of a fence post for later collection efforts.

I go to my grandparents' house at night for my mom and her sister's birthday party. Irish twins, born a little less than a year apart, they grew up celebrating together. My aunt is the younger of the two and came out tough with black hair, looking like a monkey. My mom came first, blond and sensitive. We fill the house and talk for a long time: cousins, second cousins, aunts, uncles, kids, and parents. My grandmother tells me, "I resent being this old, it's the life cycle. It's what happens to you. I'm jealous of people walking down the street, their heads held high, good posture."

Her friend told her, while driving fast down the highway, he looked in the rearview mirror and saw a skeleton in place of his own reflection. His doctor said his heart probably stopped, momentarily. But my grandmother says the friend is a writer, a fabulist.

"I'm just sad I stopped having flying dreams," my grandfather says, his hand around a can of Heineken. "Do you guys have flying dreams? I could fly. This was before my fascination with pelicans, which would have changed how I flew in the dreams."

My grandmother says she never dreamt she could fly. During the war she dreamt of the shadow of an enormous eagle bearing down and engulfing her in darkness as she walked along her street.

By midnight, when the party is over, the moon shines full. My grandma hobbles outside, propped between my mom and me, to look at its face. We round the back corner of the house beneath an ancient pine tree. The sky is gleaming, fuzzy gray and lit up, but there is no moon at its source. We cross into the neighbor's yard, thinking the distant glow is harboring the moon there. "Where's the moon?" my grandmother says, looking up. She waits for a moment then cries, "Fuck the moon!" before turning to go inside, stumbling against my mother.

My grandma tells me again how terrible birth control is. It's not that she's religious, but no one should have to make such a difficult decision paralyzed by their own free will. Also, there should be more babies in the family. She gives me a bag of her and my grandfather's XL T-shirts to bring home to Graham.

Inside my grandparents' old house, there is no time, and the light from the moon-haunted sky shines down, casting an impersonal glow upon all the jumbled generations, past and present. I eat a second piece of birthday cake covered with a yellow frosted rose, forgetting really who I am amongst them all. I am often called the wrong name, or my past is swapped with my mother's, but it all seems true enough. My grandfather, the one who changed all the diapers, eats a piece of cake with me while leaning against the kitchen counter. Even though my grandma has him off sugar, it would be bad luck not to eat cake on a birthday.

The next day I return to the pigs and dump apple mash from cider making—the sugar from the apples turned so quickly, it is already covered in drunken wasps—into their pen. The pigs will soon be drunk too. I let Gudrun, thin and limber, chase me through the fresh goldenrod. Her pink body sticks out from the tall plants, and when she finds me, she violently rubs her ears against my rough pant legs. Theresa and Ursula, focusing wholly on the apples, become wobbly and inebriated. Their wet chewing of the mash slows before they fall on their sides and succumb to sleep.

I go to Tractor Supply to buy insecticide. Looking through the aisle of dewormers, mastitis spray, and penicillin, I can hear chicks chirping from the in-store brooder; they're on sale for a dollar each. I read through the labels on different spray bottles and shakers. A woman nudges past me with her blond, freshly shorn son, cleaned up for school, which has just started up again.

"You have horses?" she asks.

"No, pigs with lice."

"Oh, I'm sorry."

"It's not so bad 'cause there's only three of 'em, not a giant outbreak."

"Good luck with that," she says sympathetically, wheeling her cart with her son inside down the aisle of equine supplies.

The livestock insecticide I buy comes in a shaker can like Parmesan cheese and is applied to the ears and back to kill insects on contact for thirteen dollars. It kills the bugs by sucking all the moisture from their bodies so that their cells break down, and it has to be reapplied ten days later to kill the eggs.

I bring the sprinkle can into the pig pen and quickly dump the powder on the pigs' heads, red spotted ears, and greasy backs. Ursula's splotches change from black to white. The can says, "Apply 1 oz. per animal," but it's impossible to measure with the pigs circling around me and rubbing their itching necks hard against my jeans. It is easy to coat Theresa's broad back, but more delicately I dust the angry red skin behind her ears and the nervous top of Gudrun's pink head, careful not to touch her brown human-like eyes. They barely notice as I turn them ghostly white.

After treating the pigs, I go into the house and find two shrews laid out nose to nose, their noses small and perfectly sharp so that they look like arrows pointing toward one another: here is our end. It seems like an attempted message from Snowman and Valentine, who kill something almost every day now. Frogs in the basement, chipmunks left on the doormat, and field mice with long tails curled around small bodies. I fling all of it, democratically, off the back deck and out of sight into the tall grass. The cats catch and eat flies too.

Only two days have passed, but the pigs look healthier. The bugs that attach themselves in cross shapes are gone. And Gudrun's hips have begun to fill in, flattening from their concave shape, so that instead of a sick animal she starts to look like a miniature one, a head shorter than her sisters. Because I see Gudrun habitually when I deliver buckets of food to the pigs, neither her wasting nor healing comes as a surprise, yet I don't wholly register the gradual change. The same path to the pen traversed daily. Cafeteria leftovers dumped from a garbage bag—spaghetti with red sauce, chicken drumsticks, kale stems, and watermelon rinds piled in the dirt.

Ursula's snout makes contact with the soft pile of noodles and vegetable peels; her head points down, and the twin black splotches on her forehead move with her chewing. Gudrun discovers the drumsticks first, running from her sisters behind a tree. She puts one hoof on the chicken, pressing it down into the dust, and rips strips of meat from the bone that disappear down her snout. Soon she is crunching bone and there is nothing left. She goes back to the pile, efficiently rooting out each of the drumsticks and eating them in secret. I believe her hunger for meat is part of her healing. Theresa takes giant mouthfuls of spaghetti; the noodles run down her chin, and her hocks are sprayed in red sauce. They eat and eat until Theresa flops over and closes her eyes, her body now the shape of a bell, convulsing with the hiccups that come from eating so fast. Gudrun's small hams mark her with a false youth but one more rightly piggish than before. And Ursula, firmly between them in size and class, allows her one blue eye to proprietarily rove the compost pile while she chews efficiently. Every so often they pause, parsing out a birdcall or the crash of a squirrel through the forest.

With autumn, all three of the pigs' hair has come in glowing white; like thistle gone to seed, it is opalescent. Theresa, lying near the mass of foodstuff, looks at me. I touch her nose, grab her ear, and feel her stomach, hot to the touch in digestion. She flops over onto her other side to be scratched evenly, grunting softly with pleasure. Her eyes close into slits so all I can see are the whites. Her wet nose and the fine hairs on her snout catch in the light, making her look like a wizened mouse. Their similar characteristics, I think, point to some kind of universal goodness across the animal kingdom.

φ

As the seasons shift, repetitious driving rain dislodges the leaves on the trees and blows them across the farm fields in rattling sheets. The yellow are the first to go. The sunflowers and dill turn to brown stalks. Living things grow more slowly or are culled in their prime and packed away. Weeds emerge between vegetables with less rapidity. With the slowed fecundity, the greens become more vibrant. In the days of gray-skyed October the cabbage patch looks electric. As if glowing from an inner light, the strange waxen leaves shine from the field.

With nightfall the first frost comes, hardening the soaked earth. By morning, all of our peppers have shriveled on their stalks and the horses are running wild circles in their pasture with no grass to eat, just frozen sod. The pigs are still asleep when I check on them. They look like three logs in a row. They are in such a deep sleep keeping one another warm that they don't wake up to the sound of grain falling into their bowls. They yawn lazily and press their noses to the palm of my hand before falling back asleep and waiting for the day's thaw to set in.

By the waxing sun of early afternoon, with everything edible in the pen sucked up, the pigs escape into the neighbor's lawn. They walk through a bed of burning coals dumped from a woodstove and are unharmed. Red sparks fire around their hooves before they lower their snouts into the embers and eat the mineral-rich wood ash.

Theresa's head has grown thick, ringed in fatty jowls. When in motion she looks as if she's underwater, face and neck rippling. Stomach lengthening, hams rounding now. Teats stretched and legs spread further apart, balancing the new expanse of body. Ursula is fat, too, and Gudrun has taken on the right shape, diminutively. It is unclear if she is healed or has just persevered.

XVIII

The Reaping

Autumn 2019, New Lebanon, NY

With the potatoes, onions, and squash out of the field, the root harvest begins in earnest. I fail to record most of it; instead it is done blind, lost as it happens. "You just remember the offal of it all," Sarah says. On harvest mornings, one after the other, I almost feel hungover. Always I wake up with a dry throat, needing more water. Thighs sore, arms vibrating, my fingers feel as if they've been pressed beneath the toe of a boot. In the dark bedroom I put heavy jeans on over long underwear and pull a wool sweater over my head, reassembling the pieces of my work self from the naked bed. It is like a sickness, this drawing out from the land.

At night I dream of what was picked the day before. My arms pinned beneath me in sleep are still working through a field of radicchio with a red-handled knife, or pulling up another of radishes until all that is left is a moonscape of ripped-off radish tops. In the dream, I move with the rhythm of them coming out of the ground, the cool feel of leaves.

Root harvest is the hardest work of the year, pleasurable in its finitude when the weather turns cold, and the reaping heavy and repetitive before the stoppage of all work and growth. Our fingers crack as their moisture is sucked away by the dirt's thirst, and our faces, bathed in the day's cold, become flushed when brought inside. As the pigs fatten, we grow harder, all of our energies funneled into the harvest. Jess wears suspenders to work because her pants have become so loose.

The first beet hits the bucket with a thud, but the sound is quickly muffled by more beets dropped inside. Each leafy green top is twisted off until our thumbs and forefingers are soaked magenta. The dead leaves that have begun to retract and turn brown are the hardest to break away. They must be carefully plucked after the green tops are torn off so that they do not cling to the beets, softening further to slime and spreading rot amongst the careful sequestration of sugar in hard globes while they sit in storage.

I crawl with a bucket in either hand, stopping on my knees at each pile of uprooted beets. One bucket is for the uniform and salable, the other for seconds—the tiny and the huge. Green leaves cover the ground behind us as we pick. We work fast, over and over twisting and dropping with trained eyes that select, with a nearly bare consciousness for grade and quality. The buckets fill up quickly and I have to carry them to the edge of the field to dump into sacks before trudging back out to my spot in the row, my heavy rain pants swishing as I lift boots thick with mud. The dog barks at strangers and the deer that come to eat apples off the nearby trees. Talk helps pass the time. As we work bent in the mud, conversations trace who's gone where, done what. What you ate for dinner. The failings of boyfriends or girlfriends, books read, movies watched, family plans, holidays, seeds, how to better farm (what went wrong crop by crop), the mice, the rats, the dog.

After work, Ethan and I drive to the edge of the Orchard of the Prophets. The orchard consists of overgrown fruit trees the commune planted and no one tends. People like to say there could be pears or apples or plums right here, but without imagination it looks like goldenrod and a few skeletal twigs. We walk below the orchard to where the pond spills out into a creek. The creek is so covered in watercress that it looks like green carpet from far away. Close up the water is clear with swaths of cress growing through it. The cloven leaves are waxy and taste strongly of peppered plant matter. With a knife I cut cress while the water circles around the ankles of my boots. Ethan climbs onto a rock to keep dry while reaching into the stream. He fills an upturned hat and an old shopping bag. Usually we find cress only in spring, growing during the cool prelude to summer. But in the strangely warmed October days, it grows just the same, still carrying something of spring's wild essence in green concentrate.

Alongside the wild greens, I bring home a crate of softened tomatoes in my trunk and bags of cultivated vegetables for the food pantry at the church, where I pass the Virgin with candles in blue and red glass lit at her feet. The woman who runs the pantry tells me of the people who come in, "They're real meat and potatoes people. No one wants the kale except maybe to feed their chickens." She keeps the pantry tidy and well stocked as a general store. Outside there's a big garden with sunflowers and saplings lashed together into tepees for string beans to grow up. There is another Virgin Mary across the road from the garden, mirroring the one in the grotto. She's surrounded by wild thyme, except for a footpath through the green and purple flowers to get to her. Footfalls bring up the smell of the plants, the same scent that burns from the cemetery and the old bottling plant, all grown over with thyme. Her cloak is lighter blue than the sky. Stumps of a cut-up sapling threaded on thin chain hang around her shoulders and fall to her feet with a silver Jesus dangling from the end of the rosary's raw wooden cross. On the ring of concrete surrounding the Virgin, names are written in white pebbles: ABBY ANNA ALEX + TARA.

Cars pass by in both directions with a whooshing sound that makes it hard to think or pray. Behind the Virgin is the wild forest, depleted by logging and hung with vines. The man who built the grotto here said he did not believe there was a reward to prayer. In contradiction to this a laminated article clipped to the prayer bench reported "old John Maher a local man who hobbled around New Lebanon for 11 years" abandoned his crutches at the grotto. He walked back to his car unaided and drove himself home in a Model T. Lodged in a corner is the plaster figure of Bernadette Soubirous, who at fourteen received a vision—for which this grotto and its original in Lourdes were made—of what she called by no name but Aquero, *that one there.*

Once home I go to sprinkle the pigs with more lice powder and find them happy in their fresh pasture, running through goldenrod under the lava pink of the setting October sun. Soon the flowers will go to seed and the pig pen will be topped with fluffy white stalks, like a low-lying cloud. The pigs' white-blond hair thickens and so does the horses' brown, so now both porcine and equine outlines are ringed in a layer of fuzz.

I begin to worry they won't all fatten in time for slaughter. Graham and I collect buckets of acorns from beneath a giant oak tree left to grow in the exact center of a field, but it is not a good nut year. The squirrels have gotten to them first, leaving only caps and tooth-scored hulls, or the acorns are eaten clean by bugs discernible by pinprick holes. As soon as the nuts are dropped in the pig pen, Theresa and Ursula begin the work of cracking them with their molars and extracting the meat, the spots below Ursula's ears jumping with each crack. Gudrun finds a cache of nuts rolled into a small pig-dug crater and eats them guardedly one by one. Eventually, all three do grow fat and Gudrun disappears into the pack.

Inside, I can the soft tomatoes, some of the last picked before the killing frost. I cut and core them sitting at the kitchen table with the TV going until the smell of tomatoes overpowers the room. The metallic-scented flesh has become loose and rotten as the cellular structure of the fruits breaks down from cold. We all busy ourselves saving food, but these days of sheer work are the hungriest of the year. I eat a giant hamburger and dream I am at the county fair in Vermont with my sister. We grew up near the fairgrounds and went over and over again during fair season. We watched the hypnotist perform the same routine (he made people sitting next to each other fall in love), saw the farm animals sleeping in their stockades, and ate maple cotton candy and fries with malt vinegar. In my dream, we go to the vegetable pavilion together. The table of entries is full of homegrown produce, which keeps stretching away from the eye. The tables grow longer and become indecipherable so that everything is reduced to organically colored dots and dashes. On a stage in the agricultural hall, a grotesquely muscled bull is displayed under spotlights while a drummer plays "Wipe Out." The light falls white on the sheen of the bull's dark hide. I wake up without warning and look out the window. All the leaves have been blown off during the stormy night, and it looks rubbed raw outside like a skinned knee.

The next day, all the endive is dug up with pitchforks to replant inside the root cellar. It will be forced to grow in sand without light until tight blanched heads come up, crisp and delicately bitter. All of the head lettuce is taken from the fields before the leaves can die in the cold, and bins of cilantro are cut for sausage before it too will turn to mush. But the real work of the day is picking cabbage. The crew harvests in lines bent at the waist. The outer leaves are forced off from each head with both hands and cracked away. The newly peeled orb is then cut from its stalk with a hollow pop. There is a chorus of cracking leaves and releasing cabbages. Hundreds of milky green heads the size of dinner platters are piled in lines. Once freed from their stalks the cabbages are tossed gently, so full of moisture and nutrient they threaten to split open like melons bursting after being picked. It is November, and we work at the cutting down in T-shirts. An ingeniously designed vegetable, the cabbage will look the same in January as it does now. A reliable life-giving thing. There is hardly anything rotten, just huge perfect heads. Every year a different crop is granted this stroke of success. I try not to take it personally, the good harvest, because next year it could rain too much or too little or the frost could come early. But this year the cabbage is perfect.

Sarah, Kate, and I wear hats made of giant cabbage leaves, catching the cabbages thrown to us, placing cabbage after cabbage into orchard bins on the moving wagon until they form great pyramids. We fill bin after bin with them, weighing down the truck, which quickly gets stuck in the mud and later threatens the balance of the tractor that takes them off to storage. The harvest is more than the farm can sell, but it is hard not to feel happy in the careless abundance of it all. After fifteen minutes all the bins are full and we wait in the picked-out cabbage patch for the tractor to return with empty ones. Bins travel back and forth between the field and the cooler until 5:00 p.m.

By 8:00 the next morning, I am riding in the truck, with a trailer of harvest bins towed behind. Ethan and I are joking in the front seat, saying how rich we're all going to get off the day's work. "It's easier for a rich man—I mean a camel—to pass through the eye of a needle, than a rich man to get into heaven," I say to Graham and our friend Chantel, both recruited at a moment's notice to help ferry food out of the field. "All the rewards are in heaven," one of them says from the back.

We ride out in the red truck and trailer packed with bins to pick the napa cabbage before the deer eat it. "My Sweet Lord" comes on the radio and we listen to it loud going down the farm road past the pond, whose surface is black and dotted in yellow leaves, and a communard flashing us his long white ponytail as he rides a lawn mower through his yard.

Unlike the near-perfect round storage cabbage, the deer have already started to browse the tops of these. Ethan counted ten deer in the fence driving by the other night. There are lacy networks inside the napa cabbages from where worms have eaten through layer after layer of leaf. Not all of the napa cabbage heads up, and it remains flimsy, the consistency of head lettuce. Bent at the waist, we work to harvest the napa cabbage as we did the storage cabbage. The cutting goes quickly, and it is hard to stand up straight again after so much bent work, day after day. When all the napas are cut, Chantel and I toss them from the ground to Graham and Ethan standing on the trailer. They place each cabbage softly in the large bins so they don't bruise. The sky falters from gray to blue and back again. Orange-yellow leaves blow on air currents across the field. The loose heads of cabbage flap out their leaves like chickens in clumsy flight.

"This is the best part of their lives," I say, "that moment when they are airborne."

"After their life source has been cut off and they're hacked away from the plant?" Ethan asks.

"Well, maybe they don't know they're dead yet and they've just been peeled of all the dead leaf matter, slippery and free," I say.

"It's like the Ascension," Chantel says.

"It's all very religious," Graham adds.

After months in storage, the heads of cabbage will start to lose their color and the outer leaves, peeled back, will reveal pure white cores.

After our work is done for the day, the sun sets and it is dark, truly dark. The power is out all over town except for a few businesses on Route 20. The gas pumps at Stewart's are all full. People fill cans in their trunks to power generators at home. A fleet of men in white power company trucks flows down the road, and a killing frost is coming. The coolers on the farm all shut off and the water won't flow. The pigs are thrown a few bales of hay to make into a nest and keep warm.

Graham and I go to the diner, their electric PASTA and BEER signs shining in the window to prove they still have power. Our electric stove at home will remain useless until everyone in town gets their power back. It is warm and cozy in the brown diner booth. There are families out on Friday night eating spaghetti casserole and fried chicken. Even though it's dinnertime, the whole place smells like coffee, insulating us all from the wintery darkness outside. I sit alone while Graham is in the bathroom and drink my beer. "Hold, hold me tight tonight, tonight. It's you, only you," says the radio. I go limp in the booth, finally warm and fed. Graham and I make a man out of dinner rolls threaded through plastic straws in a cross shape, using the straw to slurp beer through the hollow spine, laughing until I choke. My face is hot with the heat of the diner and the fizz of the beer, but there is still more to harvest, beyond the free-feeling lie of Friday night.

On Monday, we fork the carrots out of the field under weak sunshine that dims as the first snow begins to fall. Sarah and I crawl through the frigid mud, topping carrots and piling them in buckets. We try to work fast, but our hands ache with cold, becoming blunt and slow.

Sarah tells me she spent her day off getting her brakes fixed. "He was old and slow," she says of the mechanic, "but I tried to think of him as a brake savant. He had a belly resting on the car while he worked," she says, raising a gloved hand in front of her thin frame, extending it for the story, "and piercing blue eyes." She ran into a former farmer from the commune there getting his car worked on before going to protest an oil pipeline somewhere. She asked him how he has been doing but he said heatedly, "Who cares?" as if she had missed the point completely.

Our talk pauses, both of us feeling more acutely the cold.

"You wanna know a secret?" Sarah asks me. "I kind of love days like this."

"You sick fuck. I guess I know who I'd wanna be in a plane crash with."

"This is the best part of living!" she says.

Our plastic pants swish as we climb in and out of the truck, heavy with mud and fabric. The hills are already white. The world is snowy and different-looking than yesterday. It's so disorienting we can't figure out how big a fence to make for the horses in the white landscape.

Snowed out, we end the day early and Sarah has me to her house in town for lunch. Wet and cold, we drink whiskey with hot water poured in, mug after mug. Our cheeks burning, we drain half the bottle, wanting to forget the season coming to a head. We both lie and promise each other we'll never farm again.

Church sign: IN THE YEAR OF THE FULFILLMENT OF THE FRUITS OF OUR HARVEST.

Hardware store sign: PLANTING A GARDEN IS HOPE FOR TMRW.

The next day, we plant garlic, which is this year's harvest, split into cloves and replanted with the hope of summer. The moon comes out at three, waxing, and the line of the sun over the mountains sinks coolly. When I go to feed the pigs, they are steaming with heat from their pig pile, thirsty and cold with mud compacted against their fat sides. With a frigid hunger, they eat 150 pounds of feed in six days. Fattening up even more.

The night brings more snow, and a makeshift house is built for the pigs from T-posts, blue tarps, and straw bales formed into a kind of insulated lean-to. The light shines against the tarps that make their new walls so that the pigs are awash in blue light cast onto their pale and hairy coats. Sarah and I crawl in warm next to them. They lie and nuzzle us as if we were pigs too, pushing up their warm massive bodies. Sarah says they're nicer than any pigs she's known at this size, that maybe we should keep one and make her into a mother. "Can't we pardon Theresa?" she says. It'll be two more weeks now. They emerge from their blue hut to eat, fat as houses but still shivering with cold. I dump compost from the school for them in a slurry of navy beans, pasta, string beans, butternut squash peels, and rice sloughed over snow. They eat most of it before it can freeze onto the earth.

As the pigs fatten, the coolers in the barn become full to bursting. Wooden bins, bought used from a shuttered apple orchard, are stacked two high, tightly packed in rows that reach far above our heads. Carrots, radishes, cabbage, beets: 35,000 pounds. We begin to sell the harvest, and the flow of goods from the fields starts to bring in returns. The makeshift farm office in a corner of the barn is littered with checks and invoices, receipts and flyers.

From the pig pen there is the sound of ripping as Theresa plows a deep furrow through the earth, thawed in the light of midday, with her nose, stopping to chew tubers invisible to me. Gudrun comes to plunder her find and they smack their snouts against one another and plunge into the dirt, fighting through the fall-sweet earth. They want not their grain or the rotting vegetables but only these stringy roots. And there is a strange brown plaque in their ears and the sound of gas being passed, a constant air valve between the reverberation of moved ground. The tarp of their blue home crinkles in the wind. A clod of dirt comes flying toward me, dislodged from the earth and cast aside. The pigs are out on this temperate day. Tomorrow a blizzard is coming. In empty parking lots men adjust the hoppers on snowplows and get their equipment ready. On the radio the weatherman says, "All living creatures should be inside" tonight.

XIX

Returns

Winter's Eve 2019, New Lebanon, NY

On Saturday at the public library there is a release party for the New Lebanon farm pamphlet, containing historical facts and remembrances compiled by people in town. It is a government-funded project to help bolster support for local agriculture and includes maps of where all the current farms are located. The little periodical room of the library is overfull of people pressed against the bookshelves, a single congressman amongst them. There are cookies and coffee set out and a teenage boy playing the keyboard to accompany a slideshow of pictures, new and old, of New Lebanon. Photographs of pasture and plow then and now fade into each other. All the farmers are given little corsages made of cranberries and pine needles to pin on their shirts. The lady working the concession stand pins one on my overall strap while I stuff a lemon cookie into my mouth. The town supervisor speaks and so does the young daughter of a John Deere tractor and equipment dealer. The dealership's ads on the radio proclaim, "To all those linked to the land we say thank you." The town supervisor gives thanks for the food farmers grow and introduces a new program to help schools freeze local produce for wintertime hot lunches.

There is a raffle and an elderly lady wins the big cornucopia basket of syrup, apples, and cornmeal.

Sarah talks in front of the slideshow about the farm, Belle and Lou, what we grow, and how we sell the vegetables. I thought they would ask all the farmers to say something, but they just asked her, the young one, to speak, as if her youth could reverse the way things are aging and shutting down or simply fading away. We manage less than twenty acres and haven't replaced any of the big farms that have closed here, but there is some continuity that would be lost if all the farms left. Once there were sheep pastures cleared all through the hills, one thousand Jersey milking cows in town, and three train stops—West Lebanon, New Lebanon, Lebanon Springs—with cars to carry the town's agricultural products throughout the valley. Not enough has changed to supplant the farms with any conviction. In this still-agricultural community, there are pigs, beef cattle, sheep, and chickens; feed corn, soybeans, vegetables, Christmas trees, and hayfields.

Some people say already the farms are gone. By this they mean there aren't farms left to maintain the acres upon acres of pastureland and hayfields that were once the mainstay of the dairies here. One former farmhand told me about his last milking shift. He worked on a 130-cow dairy farm here in the 1970s. He finished milking with the farmer and went in for breakfast. From the kitchen table, while they ate and drank their coffee, they saw smoke coming out of the barn. They managed to save all the cows, but the whole barn burnt to the ground and the farm was forced to shut down. Their 350 acres of farmland was subdivided into housing lots. "The land used to be open," the farmhand said.

In the Agricultural Recollections section of the pamphlet there are records of the animals and crops people kept all over town. Maps new and old, overlaid in townspeople's minds, are delineated. Knowledge of former barns and cow yards coexists with homes and schools, differing crops or livestock that now occupy the same plots of land.

"Ashley Pratt milked 15–20 Holstein cows near Hanson's Trailer Park."

"The Decker barn was located across the street from present-day Mario's Restaurant."

"Stanley Chittenden grew corn on the west side of Lover's Lane. Primarily for livestock silage, he planted two or so rows of 'human corn' and gave permission to the residents of Lover's Lane to pick that corn."

"The total herd size, counting the young stock, was 185."

"Alan Wolcott raised laying hens and sold eggs near what is now the . . . storage facility."

"What's now swampy land near Churchill Road was pasture land."

The towheaded pig-farming family I used to work for is at the library, too. The youngest has her leg in a purple cast with matching toenail polish. The farmer's right hand is wrapped in a ball of gauze from a week-old kettle burn. "Everything on the farm is about the same," he tells me. It's funny seeing everyone under fluorescent light in the small library, as if they are magnified from their habitual place outside in the expanse of sunlight and pasture. Perhaps some of them even feel a bit proud. The woman who sells me piglets is here, limping slightly. She asks after my three pigs and tells me the sow that birthed them has already been slaughtered after her last litter produced only two living offspring. "And they are the neediest pigs," she says, always wanting something special mixed into their grain. The big farmer, who runs the largest vegetable operation in town with his sons, unable to fit in the crowded periodical room, is sitting at a table near the circulation desk. When I once went to his farm to buy his used watermelon boxes he asked me, "Who made money on the gold rush?" and, answering his own question, went on, "The people selling the prospectors supplies." He spent eleven thousand dollars on his zucchini and summer squash crop for inputs and labor this year and got thirteen thousand back.

Lydia, the beef farmer, helps orchestrate the event. She stands in her IT'S JUST A FLESH WOUND T-shirt, which she often wears to work in the town office. She's trying to sell her beef herd, scared she can't afford to feed them for another winter. Last year hay alone cost her eighteen thousand dollars, she tells me. All the farmers, some hurt, others in debt, have an almost clownish sacrificial air. Lydia has a chest freezer she says I can use for my pork this winter, for what we don't sell or trade to our friends for their work butchering. She doesn't ask for anything in return even though she probably needs it.

Graham and I set up the empty freezers in an expectant line in the basement and I prepare a final meal of cornmeal cakes for the pigs. The frosting is cream cheese, butter, and Fluff mixed together and made yellow with turmeric. Once the cakes are cool, I ice them with the springy yellow frosting. They look like buttercups placed on leaves of purple cabbage arranged in fives to resemble the petals of blooming flowers. On the face of one cake I write *Thank You* in sloppy cursive dribbled from a ketchup bottle, adding chopped beet confetti and a ring of dried shrimp around the edge. I cut a whole block of cheese into thirds and shove my pig cookie cutter through, arranging the silhouettes so that the procession on the cake face begins with just a hoof and a snout, followed by a whole body, and then a hind leg made up to look like three pigs in motion.

I make Graham hold a cake in each hand so they won't slip and ruin the decoration until we get to the pig pen. I carry three

Labatt Blue tall cans, one for each pig. He places the cakes on the ground, and as the swine begin to eat, I pour the beer into their bowl. The cakes are quickly reduced to crumb. First Gudrun tries the beer tepidly, then Theresa, who drinks in powerful gulps. She stops for a moment, staring ahead, and begins to take sideways steps across the frozen ground, haphazardly sniffing at the earth for the roots of food. I crouch down next to her. She sighs and stretches her fat ringed neck up onto my knee, resting her golden chin to look at me sideways through white eyelashes. It is that same connection of eye with the cats, the horses, the pigs. And the same vulnerable neck, like those of our late chickens.

It's snowing hard in the morning when Ethan arrives at my house, only to realize he didn't bring the right-gauge shotgun. Ben and I wait nervously in our snowsuits on the couch. The pigs remind Ben of his beloved pit bull and he doesn't know if he wants to be here for the slaughter, but stays anyway. Sarah arrives, and for the first time, Graham is reluctantly here too. Finally, Ethan comes back with the gun and we all walk down to the pig pen. I fill the feed bowls with grain to steady the pigs in place. Ethan steps over the electric fence with the loaded gun.

First is Ursula. I stand to the side away from the barrel and look not at the shot pig but out into the snow and dead reeds of goldenrod. The pig lays exposed on the snowy ground convulsing. It is different than killing an animal under the protective canopy of the forest. Without privacy or the insulating green of trees, the open ground, made more plain by the starkness of winter, looks like a battlefield. Sarah sticks the dead pig in the neck with a knife and blood pools out into the snow and mud. Theresa and Gudrun have noticed the fallen pig but after a moment's pause continue to eat from their grain bowls—this the preeminent drive of their life. Ethan stands over them and waits until he has the barrel aligned above Theresa's bobbing head. I stand behind him watching the quiet setup and see Theresa shot between the eyes. She falls instantly and spasms, the way it happens every time, the nerve impulses coursing through her heavy body. It is ugly out in the snow with death exposed like this. I feel sick to my stomach. I don't help, I just stand watching. I think I should be here as the completion of the animal husbandry job. In looking, one sees something of oneself in the dying animal, a claustrophobic sense of mortality. With the real thing, death, all distinction between us is stripped away.

Theresa's back trotter catches on the fence as she kicks out her life and pulls the netting down so that Gudrun walks past, sniffs the dying pig, and exits the pen. She then goes to felled Ursula, dipping her nose in her blood and circles back to the grain bowl before she too is shot. She rolls in the snow, seeming strongest now, and then goes quiet. They die in a wide triangle, two with distended eyes from the impact of the bullet passing through their brains. I am struck with a cold relief that it's over. It is always strange to take a thing in the flush of life like that. I look at Theresa's soft whiskered face and feel sad for her.

Ethan starts the tractor and drives closer to the dead pigs. The big body of the machine slides down the snow-muddy slope, making parallel brown skids before coming to a halt. We load the pigs in the bucket of the tractor, hefting them by the feet, and arrange two so they look like they're holding one another, before driving them, loose and jostling, up into the open white lawn behind the house.

From the bucket the pig bodies are dumped on the lawn, brown with mud. I spray them down until they turn golden, naked and new again after they've rolled and bucked through the mud. Then we begin a series of delineated tasks that will fill the rest of the week with work.

Graham thinks it is horrible to see, to perpetrate, and says he wants to leave the country. The open wound and the sound of fat convulsing. Blood pools and the animal jumps. "Our pigs," he says. Theresa had to be brought out of the pen in bursts because she was so heavy.

I look for signs inside Gudrun of poor health, fearing worms, but all I find are lungs paler than her sisters' and spotted. The clotted blood is squeezed gently from her heart before it is saved. This year, the hearts are put into sausage. I don't want to separate the animals piece by piece but instead keep them close.

After all three are gutted and halved, they are raised by hydraulics, hanging from their trotters on the lip of the tractor bucket. They will dangle there high above our heads in the cold, the six fat-white pig halves. Ben climbs a ladder with the buckets of pigs' heads and organs, to place those too in the lifted tractor bucket. This becomes a makeshift outdoor fridge to cool the meat for the night and to protect it, suspended in the air, from the dogs and wild animals. Later, when all the butchers have left, a woodpecker perches and eats from one of the pigs' sides as if it were a tree.

After cutting away the cheek meat, we bury the heads, two of them still with an eye forced out by gunshot. Theresa maintained her regal repose. I forget to check their teeth or tongues, objects of a personal curiosity about those parts neatly tucked away in life, and instead I fixate on the outer visage. The distended eyes and the smiling snout. The pool of blood in the bucket where the head ends. The soft forehead and friendly white eyelashes: all are placed in a hole and covered over with shovels of dirt. I

notice when we package the trotters, their footpads look pain-
fully pockmarked from walking over the rough and icy ground.

The sausage making takes long hours, mixing batches, waiting
for the slow double grind to course through the meat grinder,
and twisting links in my kitchen. The whole day Snowman, Valentine, and Gugli, the mutt, concertedly watch the grinding of
meat. Valentine and Gugli make off with whole chunks of pork
and eat them conspicuously in corners. The smell of garlic, herbs,
and cold wine is intoxicating. When we turn our backs, Valentine
sinks her white muzzle into the spiced meat and feeds. The animals don't know what to do with such a glut of meat; if allowed
they will feed until total satiation or further, to excessive sickness.

Ben's pit bull pried open the oven door in his kitchen to get
at the pig heart, kidneys, and lungs Ben was dehydrating for later
use as dog food. Instead, the dog ate it all in one go, shattering
the glass baking dishes and lapping up the hot organ meat from
the floor.

The lard renders in twin Crock-Pots on the porch so that we
don't have to smell the cubes of fat slowly melting into pools.
Somehow, the cats wear it dried into tacky spikes on their foreheads. Livers are seasoned and ground into pate, and the lard, fully
cooked down, is funneled into jars. The whole house is infused
with the suffocating smell of ripe fat. Everywhere—under nails,
in hair, on walls, in dishes, and on whiskers—there are little flecks
of pink flesh. We leave tubs of meat to cool in the late November air and the long-haired cat perches on top of the bin lids
protectively.

This year, Graham doesn't want to waste anything because of
his heartbreak over the pigs. Not even the bones are let go; instead
he boils canning pots full of them, reducing the liquid to bouillon
cubes of bouncy brown Jell-O. He makes can after can of stock
to freeze. He bakes bones and picks off the excess meat, which

he makes me eat. I say it has a cloying pig smell to it, squeezing it out of my taco and feeding it to the animals or else drowning it in hot sauce so I don't have to taste it. Graham can't understand why I raise pigs and don't like the taste of deep grease and bones.

I hear secondhand that someone dug up the pig guts to perform some kind of ritual or maybe to take a scary picture. When I shovel off the dirt, the contents of the hole are easily revealed: the pigs' blond-haired skin folded like blankets and their guts indeterminately mixed together in a mess of blue, gray, and pink. It would be okay if a hungry coyote sniffed out the food, but at this I am angry, as if whoever did this thinks we didn't already give the pigs the burial they're due. It can't yield results, I think, because they don't really believe, the grave robbers. The pigs were already anointed with our labor, these months of work like a penance to them. Not that it makes much difference now, I guess. In the end, the work is for our own human fortification, but there is something oddly complicit in this arrangement between pig and keeper. The pigs fatten with agreeable vigor, stay in the pen, eat the feed, and then let us take them. Everything that passes through our hands seems to meet a similarly sacrificial end. All that is planted and reared is taken systematically, leaving nothing so that next spring we are bound to begin the whole process again, a constant outcome for whoever farms the land.

The Shaker farm deacon recorded this pattern in his ledger, too:

> *A frost realized. The face of things bear a dreary aspect as there is nothing of the plant tribe left green, but is browned by the frost who generally does its work very thorough.*

The year's harvests are totaled:

Garden Produce
Beets 40 bushels. Cabbage 225 heads. Cucumbers 20 bushels.
Parsnips 18 bushels.
50 bushels Tomatoes. 85 bushels Turneps. Onions 4 bushels.
Vegetable Oysters 9 bushels.

Farewell thou year of uncomfortables

This year, the final harvest on the farm happens in the forty-degree thaw of midday. When the frozen ground briefly becomes more pliant, we pick the leeks. Left too long in winter's fickle onset, the roots are covered in a slick outer membrane of rot, which has to be peeled away to get at the good hearts. Two of us travel down the rows, cutting back the blue-green tops that hang decorously down into little shocks of fringe. Tugged from the cold mud, the leeks are gathered into piles, and the white stringy roots, clotted with earth, severed. We are blue-lipped, crawling through the partially thawed mud and snow, ineptly sawing away at piles of leeks. By three the sky begins to darken so that our orange rainproof pants and the blue-green of the leeks sparkle as if colors from the walls of a cave or crystal in dull rock. At four we quit the field.

· Winter ·

Solstice

Winter 2019, New Lebanon, NY

The full moon beams blue light on white snow. The many-houred December night is bathed in the cool unfaltering colors of early morning. The blue comes through the windows of my unlit bedroom. Graham and I are kissing. I pass his fingers and mine between our mouths. A cat jumps from the bed. My legs are around his thighs and I can feel his hard-on pressed against me. And then he's on top of me and we're fucking. Slowly in the blue light. It feels so good I am almost coming. Then Graham does, not pulling out like usual. We both let it happen. It drips out from between my thighs and we lie together quiet. I put my finger between my legs, feeling his seed drip out of me, velveteen, beside him under the moon rays, and we both slip into sleep. In the morning, still full of love, we read under the covers, not wanting to leave the warm blankets and light the woodstove. Instead, we lie there listening to rock 'n' roll while Snowman and Valentine circle beneath the bedroom windows waiting to be fed. The sun climbs over pine trees. Popping from the covers, I put on my heavy nightgown and Graham gets up to make us coffee and toast with eggs and fried leeks. We eat until we've had our fill and he takes me to get my car from the mechanic before driving off to work, where he'll hang paintings all day. Unlike the summer rush, the winter is a different kind of dream, which happens in a world of heavy white skies over white snows that send the seam between the earth and its firmament into retreat.

The farm's main function now is to hold vegetables. From cold storage, we ration them out to the stores and cooks, the markets, and the CSA, the work now pared down to washing, packing, and selling. Inside the coolers it is earthen and musty, wet with thousands of pounds of vegetables. There are aisles of cool green cabbage and grain sacks piled high, full of carrots, potatoes, and turnips, each thing tricked into a prolonged state of nutritive firmness. Turning on the lights is like a betrayal of this slumbering state, interrupting the dark exhalations of vegetables in a strange world unto themselves. From humble root cellars beneath houses to vast government cheese caves, we are no different from the mice with their sadly optimistic stores of cherry pits or corn kernels.

In the winter we become public, out of our fields and into the world to sell the harvest. Jess and I go to Walmart, shopping for new market supplies. With the farm credit card, we spend four hundred dollars on folding tables and tents, a lockbox for cash (after getting robbed again), chalkboard paint, and pads of invoices. Waiting in line, our winter coats unzipped because of the artificial heat blowing through the store, Jess and I read *Woman's World* off the magazine rack. There is a double-page spread on how to give a farmers'-market-themed party and another two pages on communicating with angels. There's a story about a woman's dead mother appearing to her friend in a dream; she wanted to tell her daughter to wash her pantyhose. The sentiment of it makes Jess all choked up, and she kind of starts crying in line with our shopping cart.

The holiday season is upon us and people want the show of tables laid heavy with food. Jess and I spend our weekends driving between western Massachusetts; Troy, New York; and New Lebanon. We set up and take down crates of vegetables on folding tables with chalkboard signs propped in front of our little red cashbox and vegetable scale.

The Troy holiday market is in an unheated and half-abandoned mall atrium by the big Hudson River, quieted by a busy road and the cement honeycomb of the Uncle Sam Parking Garage. I don't like it in Troy, mostly because business is bad. The women who shop at the market wear leopard-print coats, and each has her hair styled and formed into the hard-looking shell of a nut; none of them want to buy vegetables. We travel to the market in the early morning with road signs flashing winter storm warnings along I-90. We haul our turnips, radishes, potatoes, onions, green cabbage, garlic, shallots, bunched leeks, and kale to the city. There are holiday craft vendors set up all around us selling bouquets of dried flowers, tacky signs, felted finger puppets, homemade bibs, maple syrup, and eggs. Two women in matching plum-colored coats build a little stadium of Bundt cake in plastic boxes around themselves. In three hours, we make ninety-six dollars.

With no customers, the maple syrup guy comes over to talk to me and Jess. He is here with his teenage son, who sits in a folding chair in his work boots eating a large bag of potato chips that will soon be burnt off in hard work. They have a dairy farm north of here where they keep sixty Holsteins and four Jersey cows nice enough to lead around on a halter. "The Holsteins," the dad says, are just "mean milking machines," the industry standard. I ask him how they're doing with the business. His family is German, stubborn, he says. They've been farming in this area since the 1700s and just won't give up. It's not about the money. He makes alfalfa hay, grows corn for silage, and has a sugar bush that yields maple syrup and maple cream plus some laying hens: all of it a latticework of survival.

As predicted, a storm is starting, and Jess and I scurry to get everything packed up, the mountains of unsold vegetables back into their crates, and all our chalkboard signs and burlap table-cloths piled up. We leave two hours early and drive out onto roads already soft with snow. We slowly cross the bridge over the black Hudson River and fishtail onto 787 before I switch on the four-wheel drive. There are eighteen-wheelers, Buicks, and other pickups all driving forty on the highway. The world, changing from city blocks of apartments and gas stations to country roads of bare trees, is temporarily cast anew, everything muffled and anointed in fresh snow. I watch the tire tracks disappear into the white in front of me and we climb up into the hills steep and curving around the Kinderhook Creek and back down to the Lebanon Valley. Jess sits beside me in her winter hat with the flaps down over her ears and watches the road too, as if both pairs of our eyes could keep the truck from skidding out.

The following market is much the same, except that it's the annual Victorian stroll in Troy and people walk amongst the tables of wares dressed like the industrialists who used to rule the town. Couples in top hats and bonnets, kids dressed as Civil War sol-diers (Yankees), men as General Grant; women wear hoopskirts, bustles, and fur coats. Not knowing the town well, Jess and I agree we think of the moneyed people in Troy as holdovers from when it used to be the "Collar City." Now only the brick factory buildings and the river remain.

Our stand is next to the newly erected Christmas tree with branches from other trees stuck between its drooping ones so that it looks like it's not dying in the middle of the empty mall near

Christmas. Jess and I drove here in the clear ten-degree morning. Every plant, blade of grass, twig, and remaining leaf covered in glassy ice, hard and shining.

I watch Uncle Sam walk by, then an assortment of kids and teens in sashes that say MISS UNCLE SAM or LITTLE MISS UNCLE SAM. Beyond our stand of root vegetables and cabbage pyramids is a clearing on the tile floor in front of a blue-green fountain, which has been fashioned into a makeshift stage. A troop of twelve- and thirteen-year-old baton twirlers comes to perform there. The tallest girl, with a severe bull cut, starts the show off to "All I Want for Christmas Is You" playing from a PA manned by the coach sitting on the fountain's edge. She throws the baton, twirls, and catches it, anticipating its weight in her hand. She does the steps in a perfunctory series of embarrassed and jerky movements. Every time she drops the baton she bites her lip. The rest of the troop joins her on the floor. There is one boy in the group, with braces on his ankles and a padded helmet. He marches in place and raises his baton on cue while the girls spin, toss, and catch their shining batons behind their backs. Their brown and blond ponytails flash under the mall skylight. More and more people stop to watch, so that our booth is buried in a sea of spectators, who sometimes turn and look questioningly at our bins of turnips and knobby celeriac or giant white daikon radishes. The best routine is set to "Oh! Pretty Woman." They toss the batons back and forth to each other and weave in and out of line, making X's and figure eights across the floor. The music fades every once in a while when the coach gets a text on the phone she's DJing with.

After the performance is over everyone stops in front of the drooping and decorated tree to get their picture taken. The kids, given the best the family has in new winter coats and jeans, are photographed by parents with missing teeth and old shoes, a tired look across their faces. Most people don't buy vegetables. The market itself, a failure, magnifies our own unimportance; our fellow countrymen are fed by big farms, the food waiting for them peaceably on supermarket shelves. Jess and I trade a purple cabbage and some onions for a wheel of cheese, and we give the father-son dairymen carrots and onions in exchange for some eggs and a half gallon of syrup so at least we will all be fed. It is our last day's work before the new year.

My family's seven-fish dinner comes on a day of beautiful sun. It is the Italian tradition for Christmas Eve. All morning Graham smokes fish out on the back porch. I sit with him in the sunshine wearing a big wool sweater in a chair dragged from the kitchen. It is nice enough to sit for hours. I feel like some old Scandinavian and we eat our lunch with black tea outside.

After sunset, Graham and I drive to my grandparents' house for fish soup, smoked fish, shrimp, calamari, anchovies, and fried smelt with lemon—missing the seventh fish altogether. In the old days, there were live eels in the bathtub. Sarah comes for dinner too even though she doesn't like Christmas very much. She looks beautiful in her black sequined blouse and my grandmother says she looks like a woman out of a Pre-Raphaelite painting. One year at dinner my grandfather lifted his shirt to show us a bite-mark-shaped scar on his chest from a fight in the army.

This year, my grandparents tell the story of when my grandfather briefly worked as a vacuum cleaner salesman. He got the job only because my grandmother didn't want him to go to Port Chester drinking every night while she had to take care of the baby ("you went most nights too," he says). Every morning all the salesmen gathered and, humiliatingly, had to sing a sales song together. In the 1960s a vacuum cleaner cost five hundred dollars; just for allowing him inside, homeowners were given a silver-plated fork and spoon. And there was "the rocking horse clause"; the company made him tell housewives if he sold just one more vacuum his kid would get a rocking horse. One day he spent three hours at someone's house. The guy was a musician and they just listened to records together, after which he told the guy not to waste his money on a vacuum. He sold three vacuum cleaners that summer, two of them to relatives.

In the living room, the Christmas tree is so huge the top had to be cut off so it could fit squarely stuffed below the ceiling, and it is drowned in shining tinsel and big hot bulbs of twenty-year-old lights in bright colors. There is a real beauty to it, the tree hung with funny ornaments. Like when the apple trees bloom in spring, the whole house is sweetened with the smell of its sap.

XXI

A New Year

Winter 2020, New Lebanon, NY

On New Year's Day, I wake up on Ethan's couch after a night of chocolate cake and Roman candles, people falling into the snow. At midday, as the light outside vacillates from white to gray, we go out for a walk, a whole group of us who came to celebrate together. We go through the woods on the parallel ruts of what used to be a road. Ethan shows us a tree that was hit by lightning, with the bark cracked open from crown to root. Looking closely into where the bark has peeled, you can see a clean seam all down the trunk. We emerge from the trees through a tangled web of blue sap lines tied between maple trees, which mark the border of a kind of juvenile detention center on an old Shaker homestead. Like the Shakers, all the boys there work to get better. There are two empty Shaker houses and a stone barn, another Shaker settlement I never knew about hidden through the woods. Their pear and apple trees still stand in the yard. A redtail dips into the clearing following above us, flashing us her white stomach. We cross back into the woods to see the spring the Shakers diverted for drinking water. It is square and lined with stones around the shadowy water. A tree at the water's edge has bear-claw marks across it, and the dogs with us, excited by all the signs of wildlife, roll in fox scat. We find raccoon tracks over snowy logs and then the tracks of two creatures overlapping turn to blood in the snow in three red pools.

At night, I dream I am swimming in the spring the Shakers drank from. Dark and cool, it has no bottom. I see the huge black bear that left its claw mark. I sight his outline, but he quickly disappears, so I doubt if he was ever there. He sinks into the water, submerged and gone a moment, then surfaces, paddling through the pond, his fat floating him along in perfect buoyancy. He is swimming with me now and I am not afraid.

Later, I have a pig nightmare. It is a recurring one, this dream of a failure to thrive and a failure to shepherd. I buy a half dozen brown and black spotted piglets, my favorite kind. But then, somehow, I forget the lot of them. I don't feed or water them for days and leave them trapped in their secluded pen to suffer. I come back and they are half dead, their hides dried to raisin, and their bodies together in a violent heap like a bunch of discarded briefcases. Everything wasted.

Here, churches are used for everything. They are where whole towns go to vote, worship, keep food pantries, tend community gardens, and host plays, AA meetings, and harvest dinners. In Pittsfield, the farmers' market happens at the church all winter long, when it is too cold to stand outside in the park. Month after month the farm's vegetable stand is positioned right in front of the pulpit. On Saturdays it stinks of the rotting bouquets of white lilies from the prior Sunday's service. The sex of the flower deteriorates and the pollen falls away so that only the elongated white petals, loosely held together and smelling of ruinous perfume, remain. Elevated above the pulpit is a wooden cross and an eagle with a prayer shawl draped over its shoulders. The cross and its eagle, amidst the stink of the lilies, look distinctly American, as if they were made by Boy Scouts or some other earnest Christians, blocky and rough with the carver's mark.

My friend who went to Catholic school tells me there's scripture against what we are doing.

> Matthew 21:12–13
>
> Jesus entered the temple courts and drove out all who were buying and selling there. He overturned the tables of the money changers and the seats of those selling doves. "It is written," he said to them, "my house will be called a house of prayer but you are making it a den of robbers."

But the church doesn't mind because people can use their food stamps at the market and visit their neighbors, and the farmers *seem* like wholesome people. There is the woman in a bucket hat with rosacea who sells jellies and pickles, the young couple who bakes bread, the mom who sells meat and eggs with her toddlers, and the family of beekeepers who stack pretty towers of jars filled with golden honey. And me, with freshly washed vegetables in abundance. On slow days, I give away the cabbage and carrots we have so many of.

On my way home from the farmers' market, I stop at the CVS to buy a pregnancy test. I am late. I don't want to buy it from the Family Dollar in town, where they recognize me. I bring the unsold vegetables back to the farm, stack the leftovers in the cooler, and haul out the tables and signs. I want to take the test, but it is too cold in the snow, so I go home to pee on the stick. It comes out a double-line positive. With smiling surprise, I tuck the test into my dresser drawer to show Graham when he gets home. His eyes grow huge and owl-like with inarticulate panic.

Soon, I start to feel sick. I do my weekly vegetable deliveries with a grayish pale face, the snow pelting down from a colorless sky. I work nauseous, shuttling between the Pittsfield grocery stores, Troy restaurants, and weekend markets. For the first time, I can't sleep nights. I look out the curtainless windows of my bedroom onto the crust of snow under the moon, waxing again, blinking at its reflection and mistaking it for sun. I want to eat only cheese and bread: grilled cheese or cold cheese sandwiches. I throw the cooked vegetables I've grown like slop from my plate into the trash. I am exhausted, and on days I don't work selling vegetables I sleep on the couch at Graham's studio while he paints. Pink blood dots my underwear and the squares of toilet paper I wipe with. Later, it turns to red.

Every day for a month, I bleed. It is a January of snow and thaw, alternating brown and white. Some days the blood looks mud colored, others it is fresh red just like the pigs'. I don't clean it up well since it just keeps coming—sometimes it only drips, but it is constant. I feel like I am being washed out. For weeks, I fear something bad is upon me. And then it starts at the Saturday Great Barrington farmers' market. In a middle school cafeteria, a kid is playing the fiddle onstage while his father plays guitar.

Before the shoppers come in, Jess and I eat egg sandwiches in the parking lot, a gray slab beneath Monument Mountain. The blood flow doesn't thicken until after the market begins. My face empties of color and I bend at the waist, bracing myself against the crates of vegetables stacked high behind our display. I am rude to the fancy women trying to haggle unnecessarily over the price of vegetables, since I know they can afford it. Their mauve lipstick shapes words I only half hear while I make change and fill bags with rutabagas and bunches of kale. There are beautiful untouchable babies in strollers and strapped to people's chests and some due soon, still in swollen bellies.

Alice, my old boss from a pig farm, is here serving as the market manager. She stands behind a table exchanging money and giving out flyers. Her hair is cut short now and she's in a turtleneck stretched over a pregnant belly. Henry is here too, and the baby, only he's a toddler now, talking and with redder hair, so that he seems more real than before. He mashes his face into Henry's leg when Henry asks if he remembers me. "Are you excited about your new sister?" Henry asks, and his son presses his nose harder into his jeans. So, it will be a girl.

Working the New Lebanon farmers' market that Sunday, I fully miscarry. I am inside the wood-paneled hall of the fire station. Born of the certainty of disaster, it is a cozy room with Dalmatian-print curtains made by the current fire chief's wife. There are pictures of the sixteen fire chiefs in a neat grid on the wall and celebratory snapshots from drills in which people are lit on fire or natural gas shoots from the ground. There is a trophy case and letters of import framed and hung around the perimeter of the room. I like the official documents of merit. Some from the state police detail specific incidents the fire department responded to. One says,

> The atmosphere created by the unruly and violent patrons at Natalina's was dangerous and volatile to say the least. However, you and your company quickly responded and rendered both medical assistance and traffic control. The shooting victim sustained a life-threatening wound, no doubt his life was in jeopardy. Due to the professional training and prompt action of your EMS personnel . . . the victim survived.

Another from the state police reads,

> There was a hostage situation in the town of New Lebanon
> involving two escaped convicts from Connecticut . . . a
> local resident was taken hostage in his home at gunpoint
> by the two escapees and [this] continued for a period
> of about nine tense hours . . . under your direction your
> members went on standby . . . in subzero temperatures
> throughout this ordeal.

The vendors come in the morning to arrange their humble
wares of raw foodstuffs or crocheted dolls (someone makes mini
Yoda dolls) in a U-shaped promenade beneath the police letters and fire chiefs. Standing from the folding chair behind my
display of cabbage; radishes in purple, white, and black; carrots;
dirt-crusted potatoes; pumpkins; garlic; red onions; and piles of
shallots, I can feel the blood pouring out. My table is set up next
to the musical talent, an older woman with white curly hair. I
listen to her play "Ring of Fire" on the ukulele while I bleed. I
am the youngest woman here; many of the others have already
been through this, I'm sure.

I shove a square of coffee cake, made by the silver-haired
woman with ten children, into my mouth, and the overly sweet
crumbs stick in the thick saliva at the back of my throat. I want
to cry but instead focus my eyes blankly ahead at a woman offer-
ing jarred pickles and the tables of soap and baked goods and
sample cheeses. I just stand there doomed like a sapling growing
in shade, selling my oversized cabbages and squash. When I can
no longer hold it in, I go to the bathroom and unleash a hot flow
into the toilet—it is pure red blood. I didn't know I had so much
to spill; it's a constant stream of warm life and it hurts so that I

bite my lip and stare searchingly at the butterfly wallpaper in the stall.

There was something wrong from the beginning, they say. If the developing embryo isn't right, your body kills it on purpose. I see the picture of my uterus on the sonogram machine—swollen into a kind of cavern, the way it's supposed to be in a pregnant woman, but there is nothing inside. The blackness wavers as the technician moves the instrument. There is a mass of cells. She clicks on the perimeter, making measurements. A gray ribbon runs along the bottom of the screen—the line that would vacillate if there was a heartbeat. It stopped growing at eight weeks probably, she says after I put my overalls back on and ask. She wasn't going to say anything, as if I couldn't see the emptiness on the screen and her wand smeared with my dark blood. She says the rest will probably come out or else they'll take it out of me like how they do abortions. "Bad sperm, bad egg."

I leave the doctor's office and see a mom with a double stroller in the snow, trying to stuff her protesting children into a sedan. I cry walking across the blacktop and into the parking garage where my dirty station wagon is parked. Maybe I will pray for another life. Pray for something to manifest. I know in my heart there is nothing to be done—it was never my choice. Nothing good comes in winter.

I continue to bleed until I start to go anemic. I eat lots of red meat, hamburgers and the moose Sarah's dad shot, feeding on life and its successes. All of January is wasted in failed pregnancy. Days of sick and sleep turned to bleeding sadness. It offers little for the thinking mind. I watch more TV, sitting by the woodstove at home, than I have in a long time. I watch terrible shows looped in unreal colors of untouchable places and times, an electric blot on the days. Some days the cats kill shrews and bring them to the door. I do the dishes and straighten up. It snows and thaws with frightening rapidity. On the farm, I help plan what we will plant next year row by row, foot by foot. All while not knowing if spring will really come.

The winter roads are unending: white lanes between bare woods. I hate walking or driving exposed on the naked cleft apart from the woods instead of enveloped in trees, stuck on the uncaring asphalt between the Private Property signs and logging rigs. The roads between home and work are all the same, brutally so, white lanes of snow I look out at from my frozen car. When I go to the farm to wash vegetables for orders, all the water has frozen. The barrel of the root washer turns and squeaks on its motored chain, full of dirty potatoes, but no water comes out. The dry vegetables thunk against the slats of the barrel before I shut off the electricity. In the empty barn I wonder if I am losing faith, faith I didn't know I had so much of. Life twists and turns and becomes ugly and dies all the time. It is routine, the failure to thrive.

Graham wants me to feel better, wants to make love, but it is wasted on me. Two friends come to visit from New York City, but my brain has turned to rind and I feel embarrassed to speak. I don't tell anyone about the miscarriage. I drink wine, beer, and Coca-Cola mixed with wine, which my friend says they drink in Spain. We listen to music on the stereo. I want to feel free—I feel unfree, like a woman drinking amongst men, men who aren't thinking of babies or bleeding as they sit and drink. I feel rough and stupid, stupid for believing in any of it, nature's redemption.

At first, I did not think of miscarriage or consider a pig would falter from its designated path. My cracked hands curled around a beer bottle look coarse. I want to disappear into the civilized world of books and abstract ideas or its untethered opposite, memories of fucking to the albums we are listening to played so loud in my bedroom that I couldn't hear anything else. I used to think if I could become like them, men, it could protect me, but it can't. On the farm, women can't hide amongst them either. I know one farmer who lost her baby from the sheer force of hard work. Another was laid up on bedrest for a whole season of pregnancy; one went back to work too soon and got a prolapsed uterus. One farmhand took a job in the field only to show a few months later, though her male employer pretended not to notice. A teenage farmhand got sick every morning in the strawberry patch until she stopped coming to pick. I stay up late drinking at the kitchen table.

The next night, recovered from our hangovers, we go out. At the Gallup Inn, the bartender is visibly pregnant, her stomach tightly stretching her black T-shirt behind the bar. She summarily rejects us from the bar. Twenty years younger than most of the patrons, she looks between me, Graham, and our friends; one has long dark hair falling over his glasses and into the collar of his trench coat, the other wears a *too* clean outfit and is quiet from beneath sardonic brows. She inspects one of their state IDs and says, "This is expired so I won't sell you anything." My beer sits already poured behind the bar, where she was guarding it with the suspicion that there would be something deficient about us. As we leave, a man on a barstool exclaims, "You're all so tall!" while feeding his dog pieces of a relish-covered hot dog beneath the bar.

The fertile beer pourer won't have me. We go back outside to the February night, the pockmarked lot, and the barren trees. "Maybe she's in a bad mood 'cause she's pregnant," I say. "I don't usually look down at people's stomachs," my friend in the trench coat says. We drive on in the dark to a bar in the next town, an old inn where the bartenders and waitresses are young and virginal-seeming and they don't care who you are. Round trays of beer waver atop their thin inexpert arms as they lift the golden glasses off and place them on our table.

The next day, while ordering seeds at Ethan's kitchen table, I get a call from the doctor. "You can get the procedure or wait to bleed out," she says. "I'll wait," I say into the phone from his pantry. More will come and it will hurt she tells me, there should be chunks of dead cells. I can accept the no-child as long as it will stop, this time between producing and when the body tries to clean itself out. By Valentine's Day it finally ends in a night of vomit and blood.

On the snow-killed farm all the seeds we'll buy for acres of fields fit into a single filing cabinet in the barn. The remaining vegetables we bring to market are packed away in dark cold refrigeration: root vegetables, the nutritive source harvested and cut off from reproduction. The seeds have transcended the fruits and roots and folded back in on themselves. In quiet manifestation, they collapse down to the compacted source inert. From this small pellet, there is the possibility of life blooming and fattening as if it were a great accordion unfolding.

XXII

March

Winter 2020, New Lebanon, NY

Birdcalls begin at dawn again. Belle's and Lou's coats, still winter-thick, grow warm beneath the incrementally lengthening day-time sun, and their hoof marks scar the tired brown snow of their winter run. Sarah and I begin to fix the slack and snowy fences, screwing together snapped poles and refastening loose wire. The Shakers spent March much the same way, sawing wood and making repairs; lime was bought for the fields and excess potatoes sold, the sugar bush tapped and sap gathered. "Farmers mending fence & wall," they wrote in 1860. I gather trash from the field: broken shovel handles and fence posts and tractor parts forgotten in the once tall grass. We pick the kale in one of the field green-houses. White Russian, a cold-tolerant variety planted in fall: the plants have begun to regrow in ragged rows of green and the leaves are sweet with stored sugars. A taste of false spring in snow. Any vegetation on the exposed fields was all mowed down by deer long ago. Amidst the dormant landscape, the farmer we get hay from says it's already groundhog mating season. For lunch I take a mound of chickweed from a corner of the greenhouse and one scallion and eat it with a boiled egg. They are my first greens and taste of bitter dirt and weak sunshine. It is warm enough to eat outside my house and listen to the ice drip from the roof. The cats find me and lick the egg yolk stuck to the sides of my bowl.

"Joseph exhibits a wild cat that was shot on the west mountain by Frank Goodrich," the farm deacon wrote. "It measures about 3 feet & has a short Tail & is of a yellowish color." Then he reverted to his role as scribe of the temperamental March weather, "We see some beautiful Northern Lights this morning. Storm impending."

"Snow & rain today for a change in the weather" was a common refrain.

It hails at night, but by morning everything at the farm is re-covered in snow. We still have to wait to work the field. Sarah, Jess, Kate, and I work in the greenhouse, starting trays of kale, broccoli, basil, and cabbage, tricking the season into beginning earlier. The snow slides off the barn roof in loud thuds that make us jump. We discuss what vegetables there are left to sell. There are no more carrots or potatoes, the garlic is rotting, and the onions have begun to sprout.

Without any permanence, midday mud overtakes the snow, and I can hear water thawing in the ground. The plot where the Shakers kept their kitchen garden is so waterlogged the tall trees that grow there incrementally pop out of the ground and fall over, their intact root systems fanned out and the long straight trunks thrown perpendicular against the earth. Slowly they are cut up, one by one, into firewood.

On a rainy forty-degree day Lydia calls around ten to say her cows got out, could we come over? We drive in the farm truck to Lover's Lane, from which we can see a pair of handsomely turned horns sticking out from the bare bushes (Lydia doesn't dehorn any of her cows, but one in the herd has a fresh stump and dried blood down the side of her big square face from where it was recently knocked off). Behind a neighbor's house, twenty of the herd are scattered, black-and-white-mottled hides crushing through multiflora roses and dead vines. One recessive red coat stands out from the rest, and the March calves softly scamper between the less adroit adults, stopping sometimes amidst the chaos of escape to latch on to an udder. "Look at that little itty-bitty one nursing," Lydia says, pointing to a calf so white and new her coat is blazing against the field.

Appropriately, Lydia is wearing her red shirt today and carrying a long stick. The rest of us make our bodies big, holding our arms out wide and gently herding the cows back toward their gate. They travel in wide confused arcs to their familiar cowpath, bellowing at the unescaped cattle still inside the fence, who bellow back. Lydia worried they'd walk out to Route 20; they have before, crossing the road at dusk, just as the speedway crowd let out, and holding up a long line of cars. "I got all of 'em but one on a trailer," she tells me. The final cow almost got hit by an eighteen-wheeler, but she survived and came home too.

Once the cows are herded into a narrow path between fences, Lydia follows them to a bottleneck and closes the flimsy gate behind her so that she is thickly surrounded by cows. Anxiously, they mount one another and butt at each other's sides. The animals look thin from winter, their hips pointing out. Lydia says they're too rough to bring to the slaughterhouse right now. I watch from the top of the path as their heads crest a sea of long backs with one wild brown eye on each side. Lydia's red shirt weaves amongst the massive bodies. She holds her arms out, flapping her hands in command. She waits for fights to move out of her path, edging slowly toward the gate and finally opening it so the cows can go back into their paddock. The calves, with their tails spiked like dogs' in consternation, walk slowly through the manure of the barnyard toward enclosed open ground and begin to run. Once the animals are in, we walk back to Lover's Lane and find where the fence wire is down. Lydia says she hasn't named the spring calves yet, she doesn't know them well enough, though she'll name them based partly on their mothers' personalities. On our way back to the farm Ethan pulls over to show us where we'll open up a new vegetable field on Lydia's pastureland, since we've planned for more vegetables than our fields can fit.

The next day, when the ground is safely frozen, a truck pulls in to spread lime over a few acres at Lydia's where the vegetables will grow. The driver travels in wide turns over the open ground, emitting voluptuous clouds of white chalk that hang in the air obscuring everything before settling onto the dirt so that, for a few minutes, it looks as if the sky has sifted gently down to earth.

Spring Again

Spring 2020, New Lebanon, NY

Spring comes slowly this year. At first, the greening is tentative and thick with vermin. Rat tunnels aerate the manure piles on the farm and the rats chew circles in the floor of the horse shed, beneath the barn, and in the toolshed—all to get at some newly germinated seed or sack of fertilizer. In the field they run from the black dog who nips at their dirty pelts. Some rats fight standing up on their hind legs, so I can see them in profile, slight murine noses raised toward a wet foppish canine one. The dog chases them even in sleep, her paws twitching.

The first plants came from the dead ground razor-like. A green fiddlehead from leached sand, a purple crocus thrust violently out from the mud-bald lawn. But when spring finally does come, it is with a sigh; it seems not hard-won at all but like an easy collapse into a well-worn groove of verdancy, everything perennial and resurrected but reborn perfectly: the first unblemished leaf, the white flowers on the apple trees. I forget the ease of it in the farm fields, goading the land to yield unnaturally huge foods. Fat heads of romaine lettuce instead of small dandelions. It is strange to work so hard in such an abundant world as this.

On a day before the planting begins, I hike with my friend in the woods that stretch behind her childhood home, where she and her sister used to lead their goats on halters for picnics. We cut horizontally through the trees and straight up a ridge until suddenly the world opens to a whole hillside of ramps, eternally vernal, as far as the eye can see an unbelievable carpet, greener than any of the farm has yet become. The ramps look like lily leaves, long and thin strips of pastel green that when pulled reveal whitish purple bulbs. The smell of garlic rises from beneath our feet because there are so many, we can't help but step on them.

From the barn, Sarah and I drive out to the field together, smiling for the time wasted chugging down the road at ten miles an hour. I'm on the seat of the big blue tractor with the harrow attached to the back, and Sarah is perched against the wheel well going out to meet the workhorses. The uptick of the landscape, the pond, the Shaker gravestone, and the neighbor's sheep move along in time with the slow revolutions of the tractor wheels. The dirt roadsides have grown crowded with wild mugwort. I look at the plants, wishing on the big green plumes moving against one another in a way that looks self-possessed. Watching them, I think maybe this is where the spirit for a baby could manifest in some kind of energy kindled from green leaves rubbing. Sarah leans down to say something into my earphones and I look up to scream something back, but it's really too loud, so we give up talk and just look out at the creeping road ahead.

Sarah jumps off the tractor to water and harness Belle and Lou while I drive into the field. Opening ground is spring. Looking behind the tractor over the harrow, sunk deep, I can see the just-green earth turning over in thick brown waves. With the first gash comes the smell of soil. There will go our winter squash. Beneath the harrow, the field flits like the edge of a venetian blind from silvery green to brown.

Sarah follows behind the quick cuts of the harrow with the horse team. They do the finer work of grinding sod back to dirt and dead root. The disks they pull with animal strength cut into the sod and Sarah bounces along on her metal seat above the implement, pulled along too. Before I leave, she waves me down, the black reins of the horses bundled into one hand, to drive the roughest beds again before the horse team goes over them and the soil is worked against their backs and strong flanks.

Sarah says the horses are getting older. They have folds in their big hides that they never used to have. The horses' protective brown coats shine bright in a film of sweat and there is the soft sound of turning metal in soil and the bass thud of their hooves.

According to their records, one spring the Shakers traversed all their crop fields before planting time to sow the seeds of all the virtues. Brothers and Sisters in equal numbers covered every field with this spiritual "seed," blessing the empty ground before a single plant was grown.

On the first of May, a feast was held on top of Mount Lebanon and a table was laid with gifts from the spirit world, including apparitions of wine, manna, grapes, and oranges. The Shakers mimed eating the exotic fruits and loaves and drinking the wine. They spent hours in song and dance before spirits carried them down the mountainside.

"I know somebody who fed [his cows] every morning, but the grain was empty," a farmer once told me. No money left for food, driven by desperation rather than the Shakers' religious fervor, he poured scoops of air crazily into the barn until the cows starved. These are the kinds of strange rituals enacted by people dependent on nature's fickle providence. Fields are alternately bare and full, cursed to be tied to the repeating cycles of the seasons. The promise of impending growth and its sentence of fulfillment hang in the air. For posterity, the Shakers marked each spring in their farm records, proving the seasons' material return and with it their planting.

May 1859:

Farmers plant potatoes

they recorded, and feeling the shared intoxication of spring added,

Grass looks green and nice. plenty of music from the frogs.
Hallowing all night long . . .
Sabbath apple trees are in full bloom
The flowers of apple Merry
As harbingers of Summers sunny day;
For which our hearts should rear
To heaven a greateful monument praise

May 1860

A Brethren plant potatoes
P
P
L
E

B
L
O
S
S
O
M

On the farm in the heavy rain of morning, we plant our first crop of sweet peas and fava beans. It is a dismal gray out, and the sloppily plowed earth is slathered in compost and fertilizer, which we press the seeds into. The mud sticks to our boots and weighs us down. It is too wet for machinery, so we hoe furrows for the seed and follow behind with buckets, sprinkling green peas into the earth. We look like May Day gravediggers, but without the surety that profession brings. Instead we plow trenches for the living. The rows are planted hastily in the pouring rain, and we retreat to our pickup truck, sliding around the muddy fields.

Acknowledgments

Graham for everything. Sarah, who told me to write a book and then read it over and over. My sister, Alex. My family, all of them. The Atkins family. The Steadmans. Emma for reading my work, Genese for encouraging me for years, and many, many more friends for teaching me so much. The Richard J. Margolis Award and the Blue Mountain Center Residency. The Hortus Residency. My teacher, Michael Lesy. My editor, Tim O'Connell. Rob Shapiro, the assistant editor. John Freeman, editor for the home stretch. My agent, Peter Steinberg. The Hancock Shaker Village archivists. The Gallup Inn. The New Lebanon Library. All the farmers. The pigs.

A NOTE ON THE TYPE

This book was set in Bembo and was first used in Pietro
Cardinal Bembo's *De Aetna* of 1495.

Composed by North Market Street Graphics,
Lancaster, Pennsylvania

Printed and bound by Berryville Graphics,
Berryville, Virginia

Designed by Betty Lew